Mommy, You got this!!

Guidance from Granny

MICHELLE CHRISTENSEN

Copyright © 2021 Michelle Christensen.

All rights reserved. No part of this book may be used or reproduced by any means, graphic, electronic, or mechanical, including photocopying, recording, taping or by any information storage retrieval system without the written permission of the author except in the case of brief quotations embodied in critical articles and reviews.

WestBow Press books may be ordered through booksellers or by contacting:

WestBow Press
A Division of Thomas Nelson & Zondervan
1663 Liberty Drive
Bloomington, IN 47403
www.westbowpress.com
844-714-3454

Because of the dynamic nature of the Internet, any web addresses or links contained in this book may have changed since publication and may no longer be valid. The views expressed in this work are solely those of the author and do not necessarily reflect the views of the publisher, and the publisher hereby disclaims any responsibility for them.

Any people depicted in stock imagery provided by Getty Images are models, and such images are being used for illustrative purposes only. Certain stock imagery © Getty Images.

ISBN: 978-1-6642-2351-6 (sc)
ISBN: 978-1-6642-2352-3 (hc)
ISBN: 978-1-6642-2350-9 (e)

Library of Congress Control Number: 2021902782

Print information available on the last page.

WestBow Press rev. date: 04/19/2021

Mommies have a huge responsibility and extraordinarily little training. I am one who had little training. My own sweet mommy worked outside of the home from the time I was just a few weeks old. I had no college classes, nor had I read any books or attended any seminars that would have prepared me for motherhood. If you had a good mommy at home with you, you are so far ahead of most young mommies. This book is not a training book or manual. It's just a collection of stories from my life. They include the good experiences and the bad. My hope is that somewhere in the messiness of my life you will find encouragement and joy for your own.

When our daughter Danielle suggested that I write a story each day for the month of December, I scoffed. No one would want to read the honest, zany stories from our lives. I thought it a silly request. I didn't want to do it. Now, I must say I am excited to visit with you and encourage you by sharing my life in short story form. I've tried to be honest about my struggles. My hope is that you will be able to find encouragement in these pages. Each story only takes a few minutes to read. They are written as random short stories, because I know your time is precious, and you may only have a few moments available in any given day. I hope my mishaps encourage your heart.

I want you to know this...

Mothers are warriors, fighting for the hearts and souls of their children.
Mothers are nurturers, caring for their children.
Mothers are teachers, training the minds and hearts to be wise.
Mothers are experts on their own children.

Your responsibilities are great. Your reward will be great, as well. Take heart, God hears you. He sees you. He loves you! You are precious to God… and to me.

Thank you for letting me share my life with you!

I didn't have much training on how to be a good mommy. My mother was an awesome lady, but she had started working outside of our home about the time I was born. She worked days and Dad worked nights. I spent most of my time with Dad. Dad was great, but he wasn't a mommy. He was 50 years old and not too excited about caring for me every day. The two of them did their best, but it left me with no personal experience of how a mother would care for a child on a daily basis. Add the fact that I was quite young when we had our first child, just 18. You will see that the deck was stacked against me. I had moved from being a child to having one quite quickly. It would be difficult for me to beat the statistics and have a solid, traditional family. But we serve a big God. He doesn't look at statistics. He looks at our hearts. That's why I'm excited to encourage all mommies, young or old.

It is a tremendous amount of work to be a good mommy. There will be days you just want to sit down and cry. That's true. There are days that will make you feel like a complete failure. That's true, too. But...

Those days will pale in comparison to the days of overwhelming joy and pride in who your children are becoming. Tending and training your children is so vital! Not only is it important for your own family, but it's vital for society as well. Nothing you do in life can compare. There is NO career that can change the world the way raising good, Godly kids can.

I remember the times I felt so overwhelmed, unqualified and insignificant. It was pretty much a daily thing for me. Yet now when I see our five grown kids serving God and the people around them, I know that all my tears were worth it. I see our daughters interact with their own children and I am so humbled yet so proud of whom they have become. God has done a mighty work! He will do a mighty work in your family, too, if you choose to wholeheartedly follow Him.

Mommy, you got this!!

Mommy Moment...

I was just 18 when we had our 1st child. I knew NOTHING about infants. I remember the 1st bath I gave her. She cried...and I cried harder. It took me weeks of attempting to bathe this little human to figure out how to hold her, bathe her and keep her warm simultaneously. Those were rough days.

During those first months I felt so unworthy of her. I knew there were mothers who took to caring for their infant naturally, yet I couldn't even bathe mine without breaking down in tears. I loved holding her and feeding her, but that had its own struggle. I over produced milk. She would gag and cough...I would cry. Thankfully other parts of our days were easy. We spent hours in the rocking chair together. As I would gently rock her my fears would fade and my love for her would overwhelm me.

Being a good mommy doesn't mean you get everything right. Sometimes it means making mistakes and failing miserably. It means learning as you go. Don't beat yourself up for not being perfect. Learn, make a new plan and move on. You may need to ask forgiveness and/or cry for a bit. But I promise you your kids are worth every tear. You can rise up and overcome your fears. You can be a great mommy!

Mommy, you got this!!

Mommy Moment...

I was a "bonus baby" for my parents. My siblings are much older than I am. My mom thought she was no longer able to get pregnant... Surprise! I must have been quite the experience for my parents. I'm sure I threw them for a loop.

I was 7 months old at my first Christmas. Apparently, I wouldn't leave the tree alone. I pulled off ornaments. I tried to climb up in it. Every day I tried to get to that tree. Mom was afraid I would pull it down on myself. She tried putting me in the playpen. (Back 50 years, that was a thing) I guess I didn't like that. She said I climbed out several times. What was she to do?

Her solution?

Out of desperation and exasperation she put the tree in the playpen!

I think she was brilliant! She solved the problem. She kept both me and the tree perfectly safe.

Raising kids means thinking outside of the box, especially that box labeled "perfection". No kid fits in that box. Neither does any mommy. It's ok. God will help you find creative solutions.

Mommy, you got this!!

Mommy Moment...

When a new mom asks me, "How did you ever get anything done when your kids were little?" I know she is feeling overwhelmed. She is probably frustrated that she can't seem to 'get it together' and be 'perfect' like other mommies she knows. What she doesn't realize is that other mommies have very similar struggles. They feel just as she does.

My answer to the question comes with a chuckle. I laugh because it's implied that I 'got everything done.' Hahaha!!

Our house was always in a bit of a mess. If dishes were done the bathrooms weren't clean. If they were clean the laundry wasn't done. If laundry was done dinner was late.

One thing that helped me keep up with the housework was that I worked WITH my kids. From the time they could sit up they 'helped' me cook. A wooden spoon and an empty pan kept them quite happy as they sat on the counter beside me. Some days they sat in one side of the sink with a little bit of water while I washed dishes. As they grew, they helped with laundry by folding the washcloths and kitchen towels. At just 1 or 2 years old they made a tremendous difference on keeping up on housework, and as a bonus, our time together also built our relationship and taught them responsibility. Those were win-win moments.

My honest answer to the question would be… I didn't.

Relax, be realistic, and ENJOY the time that you get with your littles. They grow up all too soon. It is possible to have kids AND a clean house… but just maybe it ALL can't be clean EVERY day, and probably not all day long. It's their home, too.

Mommy, you got this!!

Mommy Moment...

I was visiting with friends about depression. It's tough to say, but twenty-two years ago I was horribly depressed.

Several things contributed to my state of mind; a cancer scare, financial struggles, loss of three parents in a span of seven months, business challenges, three second-trimester miscarriages, medical debt, assisting my mother-in-law and homeschooling. I felt overwhelmed and inadequate. The kids were about 14, 11, 4 and 2. Life was challenging to say the least.

At first, I felt I would get over it. I was busy. I functioned. I was even happy most days. But...in the evenings, I put the kids to bed and went to our room and cried. Maybe, I would sit in a hot bath. Maybe, I would just lie on the bathroom floor and cry. I was going to bed by 8:30 and struggling to awaken when the alarm went off. But I had a family to care for, they depended on me. So, I managed the best I could.

It was a dark time. I wasn't the mommy I wished to be. I did the best I could. Yes, I was praying. Yes, I was active in church. Yet, my heart was so heavy.

Thankfully, God broke the emotional box I had put myself in. I am so very grateful that He did.

I pray that in sharing this someone will see that they are not alone. Don't hide your hurt. Find someone you trust and share your struggle. Please know that God loves you and wants to bring joy back to your heart. Tell Him all of it, share your pain with Him. He will help you!

Mommies, if you aren't struggling, look around at the women around you. Chances are you have a friend who is hurting. Please, hold each other up in prayer, and please, talk with each other.

We need each other.

Mommy, you got this!

Mommy Moment...

Our second child, Devin, brought several gifts to our family, one of those gifts is joy…pure, sweet, innocent joy.

He was happy all the time, from the moment he got up until he flopped down to sleep. Every day his sweet smile and happy presence filled our home with joy.

At 1 year old his favorite thing was to hide somewhere, behind a door, under a blanket, just anywhere to hide. He was ecstatic if we had a box in the house. He would climb in and pop up laughing. Sometimes startling his mother, which naturally brought him even more joy.

While my niece and nephew were here for a visit, they thought he was hilarious. Several times they put him into a 5-gallon bucket, told him to "hide" just so they could watch his face light up when he jumped up. We have photos of those two holding a 5-gallon bucket between them with Devin in the bucket. The joy on those three faces makes my heart sing even today.

Each child brings 'gifts' to their family, maybe hope, faith, peace, love, or joy, maybe enthusiasm. Look for those gifts. Write them down in their baby book or scrap book. Your children will love looking back and reading about what gift they brought. If you are unsure of their gift… pray, ask God to show you the gift that child brings.

Help your children see their gifts.

Mommy, you got this!!

Mommy Moment...

As a society we have shifted. Pressure is put on women to do it ALL. You must have a career or at least a good job. You must have a college degree. Somewhere in there you should have a couple kids, but not give up your work. Being Mom doesn't carry weight as a credential.

But, let me tell you a few of my "mom credentials". I'm a chef, a nutritionist, dietician, a purchasing specialist, janitorial supervisor, operations specialist, and sanitation expert, and that's just in the kitchen! I am Doctor and nurse, mental health advisor, child psychologist, physical therapist, and behavioral researcher. We homeschooled our kids, three of them all the way through, that means I'm a preschool teacher, elementary teacher, Jr high and high school teacher. Math, history, science and English are my specialties. I'm also safety inspector, clothing designer, seamstress, housekeeping supervisor, horticulturist, gardener, landscaper, taxi driver and at times a veterinarian…

I think you get my point.

It's hard to be a mommy. You are expected to know so many things about… well… so many things. You will have days when you don't know what to do.

As our kids grew, I listened to several prominent family experts; people who had all the right worldly credentials. Although they truly were smart people, I have discovered none of them had 3 or more kids. They had an enormous amount of knowledge, but they had limited practical use of that knowledge.

Sweet Mommy, you are the expert in your home. When you don't know what to do, pray! Ask God for His wisdom. He has lots of kids, some are more obedient than others, but He loves them ALL. He understands your hurts and your heart. Hold on to Him.

All the jobs you do truly matter. They matter to your littles, but also to the world. Good mommies raise good kids. What you do is important!

Mommy, you got this!!

Mommy Moment...

Most of us struggle to keep up on housework. As I said before if one thing was completed something else was left undone. But to help me out, my dear husband took on the task of putting our kids down for naps. Which meant I had time to clean up lunch and maybe wash dishes...or sit down for a moment of silence. The kids loved it. It was a highlight of their days to get to lay down with Daddy. I truly mean that. He made it a game. After lunch they would race off to the bedroom, hop up onto our bed, and shout, "I'm in your spot!" They were so excited when they got there before him, for if they did, he'd scoop them up, spin them around and throw them back on the bed. They'd laugh and jump back up to have him do it again. He might do it two or three times and then he'd say, "Ok. It's nap time." And they would lay right down, hearts pounding, cheeks flushed. He'd ask them what the '5 ingredients' were.

They would reply… in this order...

1. Be still.
2. Close your eyes.
3. Hold my hand.
4. Be quiet.
5. Go to sleep.

And they did! He never had a bit of trouble. They LOVED taking a nap with him. I was always in awe of this routine. He wound them up, made them giggle, and yet they'd go right to sleep.

In your parenting, I'd recommend making a game out of anything that you can. Whether it's napping, cleaning up toys, or scrubbing the toilet.

Make it fun somehow and they will be happy... and obedient. And that will make you happy.

Mommy, you got this!

Mommy Moment...

I always understood that children need their daddy. Statistics prove that a good relationship with a father figure is a determining factor in success. Encouraging that relationship was a priority. God showed me several ways to do just that.

When Curt came home at night, he was exhausted most days. Farmers put in 12- and 14-hour days on a regular basis.

I wanted the kids to be excited to see him, and him to see them. So, it became a game between the kids to race to untie Daddy's boots. They'd hear him coming through the garage, and off they'd go on the run. They could hardly wait for him to get in the door! They'd run to him, push his pant legs up and race to see who could untie and loosen their boot first. They'd be laughing the whole time, so would Curt.

It is a precious memory now.

By the way, if you ask our grown kids, especially the girls, if they think their daddy 'walks on water' they'll probably say yes. He was and is their hero.

Mommy, you got this!!

Mommy Moment...

Our first two kids were (and are) good friends. They played together all the time. They had these huge Raggedy Ann and Andy dolls that they drug all over the house! If they weren't playing with those dolls here in the house, they were often out in the playhouse together.

Occasionally, I would hear them fussing at each other or arguing over something. I'd remind them that if they couldn't play nice with each other then they couldn't play together at all. Then I'd put them in their respective rooms and shut their doors. I'd return to whatever I had been previously doing… and wait.

In five minutes or less they would be sneaking down the hallway to the other one's room. After that they would play quietly and happily together for the rest of the day.

I didn't grow up with siblings in the house. (mine are much older than I am) As a parent I had no reference as to what normal sibling interaction was. I prayed a great deal about this. It really bothered me when the kids didn't get along, and I had no idea how much disagreement was ok.

God helped me see that I set the standard in our home. I got to make the decision as to what behaviors were allowed and what was not. I began to put together a list of behaviors that I found upsetting. In our home screaming, for any reason, is NOT allowed. Fighting is not allowed. Same with slamming doors or being disrespectful. Although you can be mad, you can't be disrespectful. You don't get to slam doors in anger. There are several basic standards of behavior that are expected here.

It may seem silly, but I'd encourage you to consider what behaviors you expect from your kids and make a corresponding list of consequences. Then, emotion won't get the better of you in the moment. It will bring you…and your kids…great peace.

Mommy, you got this!!

Mommy Moment...

Traveling with littles can be an absolute joy! I know that some of you could tell horror stories about car rides, but truly it can be a terrific bonding time.

We spent a good deal of time in our car. We live in the country and it is a bit of a drive into town. Plus, we are 50 miles from the nearest city of any real size. That meant we had loads of time in a car together, and there were no electronic games, no cell phones, no tv's... just us.

Often, we listened to the original Odyssey programs and talked to each other. The kids learned so much from those programs. - Not just the kids, I learned along with them. The programs gave us topics to discuss. We laughed together. We cried together. They gave us encouragement and opened communication. They helped build our faith in God.

Thirty years later I still travel with Odyssey CDs in my car. My "baby" is twenty-two! The episode entitled 'Do or Diet' is our favorite! It's downloaded on the kids' phones to this day. Yes, my adult children's phones have kid's programs downloaded on them by their own choosing.

Use all the moments you get. Kids aren't little for long. Find ways to connect their hearts to the heart of God. It will strengthen their faith and help them stand against the tide of immorality that grips so many kids.

Mommy, you got this!!

Mommy Moments...

At about four years old, although she had always been compliant, Danielle decided one day that the candy at the checkout counter looked good. She also decided NOT to accept my answer, which was no. She started to whine as I finished checking out. Just as I was paying, she had another thought. Down she went, onto the floor… in full tantrum mode.

Now, I hadn't seen her do this before. I had no "How to deal with a tantrum in a store" file in my brain. I simply told her to get up because I was leaving the store.

She continued.

The poor clerk was a bit horrified when I started walking out of the store.

I exited the store, watching her the whole time through the huge glass windows, and waited just outside the door. About then she looked up and saw that I wasn't there. She popped up and came a running. I snatched her up as she exited the store and hugged her tight. I calmed her little heart and kissed her. As we proceeded to the car. I reminded her that her behavior made me sad, and wasn't how a sweet girl would behave, but I loved my sweet girl.

She never tried it again.

Sometimes you have only a moment to process and decide what to do. There is no way to prepare for every situation. Remember, you may not like the behavior, but you *adore* the child. You will parent well most of the time but cut yourself some slack if you don't.

Give yourself and your children grace. Nobody's perfect.

Mommy, you got this!!

Mommy Moment...

One day, the younger three and I had made a "parts run" to the tractor supply store for Curt. We often helped him by going for parts while he took apart a broken piece of machinery. The guys at the parts department all knew us and were always nice to the kids. That day, one of the salesmen gave Caleb a candy. It thrilled his little 4-year-old heart! He came running to me to ask if he could eat it.

When…SMACK!

He tripped. His face hit a display and it cut the bridge of his nose!

I was only six or eight feet away from him. I jump up from the parts counter, ran to him, and sat right down beside him. His nose was bleeding profusely, and he was quite frightened by it. And naturally, he was crying.

God must have taken over because I was completely calm.

I quickly realized what was bleeding, rolled Caleb into my lap, put my thumb over the cut, applied pressure, made eye contact with him and started speaking calmly and quietly. "Look at me. Look at me, Honey. Calm down. You have to stop crying, Honey. If you stop crying it will stop bleeding. You have to stop, Sweetie."

About then he stopped crying, never breaking eye contact with me.

After a bit of assessment and rocking him sitting there on the floor, I put him in the car with his sister's and went back in to actually pick up the tractor parts we had come to get. One of the technicians who watched the incident was astonished. He said he was an EMT and had NEVER seen a kid calm down so quickly. I smiled and replied, "He trusted me."

As a mommy it's easy to fall into the trap of too many words. I implore you to say what you mean and mean what you say. Your kid's life may one day depend on them obeying you. He was in no serious danger that day, but he was quite frightened. His faith in me and my words quickly defused the situation.

Trust is a simple thing… but can be so easily destroyed by our own words.

Mommy, you got this!!

Mommy Moment...

Several years ago, we started a silly Christmas tradition. We give everyone some sort of indoor shooting device first thing in the morning. There have been homemade corn shooters, rubber band guns, and of course, nerf guns of every sort.

One Christmas Danielle and I had the great idea of giving marshmallow guns. We bought EVERY elbow and T of 1/2 in PVC in our county! I am not kidding. We emptied every hardware store and plumbing supply place in the area. We even raided the stash of a friend who is a plumber. It took us weeks to find enough pieces to make one for each of us.

Christmas morning, everyone received a marshmallow gun and a bag of mini marshmallows. I believe there were thirteen of us at the time. That's a lot of marshmallows!

It was a blast. No one was safe. No place in the house was off limits. Marshmallows EVERYWHERE!

Then someone added a jellybean and it rose to a whole new level!

Even when we didn't have a whole lot of money the anticipation of Christmas morning antics thrilled our kid's hearts.

Create fun traditions for your little ones. It will thrill their hearts. You don't need to be as silly as we are to have a good time together.

Have fun. Make amazing memories!

Mommy, you got this!!

Mommy Moment...

I hear friends say that they think I have a "natural gift of hospitality." Hahahahaha! That is a funny thought.

Oh, girls, if you only knew where I started! I couldn't cook, unless you count Mac and Cheese. I had no homemaking skills. Planning, coordinating, and budgeting were NOT in my skill set. These next few stories will make you feel good about yourself. I promise…

I was running behind and hadn't started soaking the pinto beans for the chili I had planned to make, so I was trying to hurry things up a bit. I had used the pressure cooker (old fashioned Insta-Pot) before. I knew a bit about using it…but…well… maybe not enough.

I sorted 2 or 3 cups of beans, put them in the pressure cooker, added water, attached the lid and turned on the heat. -All the right things. I knew that to regulate the pressure I'd have to turn the heat back down once I heard the pressure valve jiggle. I moved into the front room to be with the kids and listened for it…

Well, I thought I was listening. I didn't notice just how much time had passed.

Suddenly, the valve blew! Beans were shooting up through that tiny little valve spout right to the ceiling! Splattering all over the kitchen! I mean ALL over! You've heard of Old Faithful?

Oh, what a mess! Ceiling, walls, cupboards, and the floor all covered. Beans shot not only on the outside of the cupboards, but INSIDE of nearly every cupboard in the kitchen! Bean juice was inside the light fixture! It was awful. Who knew a full-sized bean would fit through a hole smaller than the size of a pencil eraser?

Stepping into that mess to shut off the burner and move the pan was so disgusting!! Once I removed the pan from the heat and the fountain had stopped, we all laughed. I think we all held our breath for a while there. It had been a shocking and somewhat terrifying sight! But no one was hurt, nothing was broken. There was no permanent damage. The next day or two, as you can imagine, was spent cleaning.

Something good came of it though. That was probably the cleanest my kitchen has ever been.

Things don't always go as planned. Don't panic...and don't give up.

Mommy, you got this!

Mommy Moment...

Have you ever made soup? I mean real homemade soup. I enjoy making soup. Usually, I start by making a broth. It might be chicken, or it might be beef. Either way, I put the meat in a Dutch oven, cover it in water and let it simmer most of the day. Then I make my soup with it in the evening.

That's how it SHOULD go, but...

It was a busy day. We were going to go into town to do errands. I hadn't thought to start the soup broth earlier, so just before we left, I turned it up a bit high...just to get it started, you know. I planned to turn it down to simmer as soon as it came to a boil.

We got ready and headed into town. Jenna, Kali, Caleb and I hustled around grocery shopping for the company that was coming. We had agreed to host an exchange student from Denmark. It was great fun planning out some meals for our guest. She would be here in less than 48 hours.

I knew what I had done the minute we turned into our driveway. I could smell the smoke!

Suddenly, I was shouting at the kids to stay in the car! Don't move! They had no idea why I was shouting or why they had to stay in the car... or who was this purple minion driving and shouting at them... or what had happened to their real mom.

I parked out front, not daring to pull into our garage. Walked into the garage. So far so good, but the smell was horrible. I crossed through the garage dreading what I'd see when I opened the door into the house. I felt the door with the back of my hand. It wasn't hot. I opened it. I could see nothing!

The smoke was so thick I couldn't see a thing. It's maybe 20 feet from our back door to the opposite wall and I couldn't see it!

I dashed in, shut off the stove, and dashed back out. I returned to the car to explain what was happening to the kids. Then, I walked around the outside of the house, opening the doors to get fresh air in and smoke out. It dawned on me that I could switch on the ceiling fans from the doorways, so I did that, too.

Thankfully nothing burned...except the beef bone.

But my poor kids spent the next 24 hours helping me clean EVERYTHING! Devin ran a carpet shampooer for hours and hours. We scrubbed walls, we washed every blanket, pillow, tablecloth, and towel. The washing machine ran continuously!

We learned 2 important lessons:

1) Pear scented fragrances cover smokey smells

2) Air conditioner filters hold smoke and must be cleaned out after a smoky event. Otherwise, when they are turned on, the room fills with smoke... again.

Jenna says I don't hold the bar of perfection up too high. LOL. That's so true! I'm actually truly pleased to hear her say this. It means my kids know I mess up, and that makes it ok for them to mess up, too.

Mommy, you got this!!

Mommy Moment...

I don't know how you and your in-laws interact. I can tell you mine did NOT approve of their sweet 20-year-old farm boy choosing a teenage city girl!

I'm not so sure his Mom ever got over it. She was good to me, but that was about it. I took care of their lawn and flower gardens and helped with housework, but I was still a city girl to Mom. Dad saw me differently. I had raised a garden with him from the time I married into the family, and I did all sorts of menial jobs for him.

He saw me work with Curt on the farm, doing the things that I could. He saw my willingness to learn anything Curt asked of me. I shoveled rows for irrigation. I hefted bales. I cared for any baby animal Curt brought to me. I learned to drive all the tractors. I raised a huge vegetable garden with Dad's guidance. -Not that I did any of it well. I was just willing.

Dad and I were working in the wood shop together, something Curt and I did with him every winter. As we were working, he seemed to be stumbling over his words. I couldn't figure out what he was saying.

It was as if he was having trouble putting sentences together. I was a bit concerned. I stopped working to actually focus on what he was attempting to say. When I began to really listen, I realized he was desperately looking for words to express the fact that although he had not been in favor of Curt marrying a city girl, I had turned out to be a good choice. He was proud of Curt for choosing well and proud to have ME as his daughter-in-law. I cried.

Even now to write this, I am crying. This took place just a few years before he died.

It means the world to me to know that this man whom my husband idolized, and I adored, had learned to care for me. I earned his respect.

I'm a hot mess. I STILL do ridiculous things and struggle to feel worthy. To know that he was proud of me is overwhelming.

Thing is girls, you are worthy! You don't have to EARN God's love. You don't have to prove anything. He is just waiting for you to turn to Him. He already Loves and adores you. He sees your heart. Maybe you know Him, but struggle as I do, its ok. He knows you. He knows me. He knows what a mess I am. Yet He chooses us if we will simply turn our heart toward Him and repent. I pray that you will hear His Holy Spirit tell you that He adores you!

Mommy, you got this!!

Mommy Moment...

When I was just tiny my eldest brother was sent over to Thailand during the Vietnam War. My folks would send packages of gifts and treats.

My sister was a young teen at the time and made a special Christmas stocking out of red felt for him. It looked a bit like elf tights.

Mom stuffed it full of Christmas goodies, and mailed it off to him. Although he appreciated the sentiment, he gave the stocking back to Mom when he returned from the war. Mom offered it to my sister, but she didn't want it either. Mom kept and treasured it.

As I grew up Mom used the stocking to hold the Christmas cards from friends and family. We didn't always decorate much for Christmas, but this stocking was always hung up.

I inherited it years ago. We turned it into an advent stocking. Curt and I put a little candy, juice or toy in it each day during the month of December, one treat for each kid at home that day.

Sounds sweet doesn't it? Well…you know how kids sometimes blurt out things. Sometimes the things they say get confused and come out in totally embarrassing ways…

Danielle's kids love this stocking. It is always so much fun to watch their eyes light up when they get to go to the stocking for a surprise. Someone at church asked them what their favorite Christmas activity was. One of them joyously proclaimed,

"We get candy out of Granny's underwear!!!"

Mommy, you got this!!

Mommy Moment...

We have several unusual traditions. – As you have just read. But there's more…

On Christmas Eve the kids were allowed to open one gift. Then, on Christmas morning, when they awoke (at some horribly early time) they found their "Santa gifts" set up and waiting for them in the front room. It worked out well because wrapping a tent or a large, homemade barn for Breyer horses is nearly impossible!

Here's the thing, we called them "Santa gifts", but the kids always knew they were the special gifts from Daddy. We didn't and don't celebrate Santa. We didn't do wish lists. We didn't encourage the materialistic side of Christmas.

…Well, we decorate everything in the house that holds still, but I mean we don't go overboard with gifts.

Instead, all the joy and anticipation centered around their father's love for them. It seemed to be a small thing at the time but looking back I see that it was invaluable to their hearts. It solidified in their hearts the fact that their Daddy adored them.

Mommies, there are few things more important to a child than knowing that they are adored by their daddy. I encourage you to find every way possible to encourage that.

Our kids are all grown up now. But still, they wake up at 4:30 AM Christmas morning to see what "Santa gifts" await them. I love that!!!

Mommy, you got this!!

Mommy Moment...

I've had a few of you wondering where Curt was for some of these stories. The answer to that is, here, of course. Well, within a mile or two of here. He owned a farm and raised cattle. He worked EVERY day. Oh, we could go be with him pretty much any time. The farmyard is about 3/4 mile from our house. As they got older, the kids would ride their motorcycles down to him quite often, and we walked down nearly every warm day.

A typical day started at 5:30 am... unless it was calving season...or summer...or fall… then it was 4:30. We would eat breakfast as a family at 6. Then he was off to feed the cattle, as many as 2,500 of them. Then there was mechanic work, field work, irrigation or building projects. He stopped for lunch about 12. We would eat as a family. He generally stayed home with us an hour. Putting the kids down for their nap after we ate gave him a chance to connect with them and to rest a minute. Then back at it he would go. By the time he had finished the evening feeding it was 6 and time to head back here for supper. Then off again to finish working. That was "normal".

Calving season for us began in January and ended sometime in March. Keeping close track of them to insure none of the mommies had any issues meant checking the cows before breakfast, before going to bed and several times in-between.

Summer ...which really means spring and summer... meant irrigating the crops and working in the fields. That added an hour before breakfast and several hours after supper. He would go out early and do all of the "irrigaty" things. Then he would come have breakfast with us. He didn't have sprinklers then. He had to haul small aluminum tubes across the fields with him as he moved to water new sections of the fields. Mealtimes stayed the same...usually...but the workday lengthened.

Fall, you already read about. When he was in harvest, he not only worked all day with everyone else, but he did all the maintenance and mechanic work before the others gathered in the field or after they had finished for the day. Those days started at 4:30am and often didn't end until 10 or even 11 at night.

We don't really understand an 8-hour workday, and animals need fed EVERY day so "weekend" doesn't mean much either. He did get a break on Sunday. Those were his "lazy" days. He only did the feeding of the animals and minimal work, so only 5-8 hours then. He'd feed the animals, come get cleaned up and head off to church with us. Sometimes we had him home all afternoon and then we would all go do the evening feeding. Other times he would go down mid-afternoon and work a bit.

Now when you read one of our stories you will understand why I often speak of just the kids and me. It wasn't that Curt wasn't here; it's just that the man worked 12 to 17 hours nearly *every* day. I am so blessed to have such a great man for my husband!

Mommy, you got this!!

Mommy Moment...

One Christmas I was looking for a craft to do with Dani and Devin. --This was YEARS ago...before Google and Pinterest. My mom came up with "peanut people." What are "peanut people"? Well…

˙I bought a large bag of peanuts in the shells and found scrap pieces of felt, narrow lace, pipe cleaners and googly eyes. We carefully opened each of peanuts, saving all the shells. We ate all the peanuts, of course. Then, we glued the shells back together. As the glue dried, we imagined a whole village full of peanut people and began to create clothes for those imaginary people, Christmas dresses, snow suits, tuxes, hats, scarves, etc.

Seriously, we created a village full of people that year. Our village included: a skier, a mother and baby, a preacher, kids sledding, a couple headed to church, and even a choir. We created a baby carriage for a mother to push around our village out of a walnut shell. It was a full scene. We used quilt batting scraps to make a snowy mountain for our skier.

Silly, right? Probably. But It's a delightful memory. We had so much fun!

It's been thirty years since then, most of the people have broken, but I do still have a few of those little people. I put them out each Christmas. They make me smile. They make my kids and grandkids smile. They fill my heart with love for my mom.

Create fun moments. Laugh together. Make memories. -Those last forever!

Mommy, you got this!!

Mommy Moment...

Sometimes I felt like Daddy got to do all the fun stuff with the kids. They loved setting water with him. They loved feeding hay with him. They loved hanging the Christmas lights on the house with him. They simply loved to be with him. They enjoyed their time with him. If I had to be gone, they were THRILLED to go with Daddy.

I knew something was up as soon as I got home. Devin was acting a little differently after a day with Dad. I didn't ask what had happened, and neither of them said anything. Devin acted as if he had a surprise or a secret he was dying to tell.

Weeks later I learned what it was that had him acting oddly. Devin had driven the old tractor from Snyder to home, a good 7-mile stretch of road.

He was 8!

Curt needed to bring a tractor from a neighbor's field back to our place. They went to get it. Devin had driven with Curt many times. He was a good driver. So...Curt had let him drive the tractor home because... well, that made more sense than letting him drive the pickup.

He apparently had done a fine job of driving right up to the point he had to turn into the farm lane. At that point he forgot to slow it down and took the corner way too fast... possibly having a tire off the ground... but He made it through the corner, learned from the mistake and never forgot again.

Curt waited weeks before he told me what they had done. He wasn't willing to frighten me, nothing could change what had already happened, and really, Devin was quite a capable driver.

I learned I could trust Curt to know the kid's limits AND trust God to watch over them.

Daddies are totally different than mommies and that is ok. It's actually a GREAT thing. Kids need both.

Mommy, you got this!!

Mommy Moment...

I see young moms in the stores. They are frazzled and not really engaged with their littles. They are just trying to "survive" the shopping trip. It breaks my heart. How much joy they miss!

Grocery shopping was our big outing. We shopped once a month. (Yes. It can be done) We kept a running list. The kids could add to it if they noticed that we were low on something. It became a part of our homeschooling. The kids were in charge of some meals, so they would add the items needed for those meals. The first of the month would come, and our list was ready! Our younger 3 will tell you I usually warned them, "You are homeschooled kids out during school time. Be a GOOD example." It was a reminder. I expected good behavior, but I made it fun to be out together.

We all looked forward to our monthly trip. We would leave the house after breakfast. The car ride was half the fun. We listened to stories, sang songs and visited. Once at the store they each had "jobs" to do. As tiny ones they sat in the cart, but as they grew their responsibilities and freedom increased. When they were old enough, I'd hand the items from the shelves to them to place in the cart. A bit older than that and you could walk beside the cart and retrieve the needed items from the shelves, and hand them to the little one riding in the cart. Truly responsible littles were allowed to push the cart. Cart pushing was a privilege. You had to be a careful driver AND be strong enough to push it once it was full.

We had fun. Truly, it was a marvelous time. If the weather... and their behavior... allowed I would treat them to a picnic after shopping. Sometimes we drove up the canyon above Loveland and we would find a park along the creek.

Littles WANT to please. They WANT to be helpful. Shopping can be a wonderful, bonding and teaching time.

I know you are stressed. I beg you not to add to the stress by being cross and disconnected.

Remove some of that burden by being intentional with your time. It really does help.

This world is a mess, and we have messy lives, but God wants to walk with you. He promises to do so. He promises to draw near to you if you draw near to Him. He promises to give you wisdom if you ask. He will help you be creative and intentional.

Mommy, you got this!!

Mommy Moment...

Danielle was probably our most compliant. Good thing, too. I was only 18 when she joined our family. I was a young wife learning to be a good farm wife, and suddenly I had to also learn to be a good mommy. I was super happy to be a mommy, but completely clueless.

She was my little doll. We were never apart. I held her nearly all day. We went for walks. We cleaned house. I even kept her with me when I cooked. It actually got to the point that she wouldn't sleep unless I was holding her.

Curt was wise -and maybe a bit tired of having her join us in bed. One night I was trying to leave her in her bed. I had changed her. I had fed her… again, checked her… again. She was fine, but she knew I'd give in. She would cry each time I laid her down. After getting up several times to check on her "just in case," I was exhausted and teary. Curt rolled over as I was getting up ...again.

He asked; had I changed her, had I fed her, had I checked on her? I answered yes, yes, and yes. I had done all those things many times, but she was crying...again.

"Then she's fine," he stated matter-of-factly. He stretched his arm out, laid it across my chest and went right back to sleep.

She cried for just a little bit but went on to sleep. I cried far longer than she did.

I had to learn when I was being manipulated and when she really needed me. It was a tough lesson, for me. I am a pleaser. I want everyone happy.

As a mommy I had to learn strength and dignity, grace AND truth. Danielle says babies have never been inconvenienced. We have to teach them the difference between their wants and their needs.

I wish I had had the adult her to help me raise the baby her.

Mommy, you got this!!

Mommy Moment...

Washing the floor had become quite a challenge. My bucket kept getting knocked over...again...and again...and again. Nine-month-old Jenna was fascinated by my mop bucket.

I like to scrub my floor on my hands and knees, which put me at a disadvantage to this sweet babe. The first time, I laughed and set her out of the room with her toys. I went back to scrubbing. She returned and did it again. I returned her to her toys and went back to my work. Once again, she dumped my bucket. We did this *many* times!

Being mommy is tough, especially in today's world. Children are either devalued or held up as idols. In so many ways Mommies can't win. If you punish your kids, you may be considered abusive. If you don't, you are a terrible mom with bratty children.

I watch my daughter, Danielle, who has 7 children, navigate disciplining her kids *so* well. I have never seen her spank a kid. I have never seen her speak a word to them in anger. She DOES expect obedience and respect. She does so by having clear rules and clear consequences. They are very obedient and extremely respectful. I wish I had been wise enough to be that kind of mommy. I eventually learned it through trial and error. It took me several years to figure it out. When I went through the 'hard years' that I wrote about previously, I was filled with emotional battles and depression, I was not always wise.

I had been a mommy for 11 years when Jen kept dumping my bucket. I had grown in my mothering journey. I saw humor and curiosity, not a disobedient act. I put the rag away, poured the water into the sink and played with my baby. The floor stayed dirty.

The wisdom to see the difference between disobedient behavior and childish behavior will make your life so much easier. I learned to set the atmosphere of our home, to be the thermostat not the thermometer.

P   y. Ask God to show you what the heart is behind the behavior.

    n's heart was joyfully childish in her actions. You can love the kid
    nd not like a behavior.

Mommy, you got this!!

Mommy Moment...

When Danielle was in second grade And Devin was four, I began to feel God pushing me towards homeschooling. God began bringing homeschooling friends into our lives. Pastors that I listened to on the radio were encouraging parents to homeschool. Curt was sure I could teach our kids, do it well and enjoy it. Yet I fought it. It frightened me. I would be responsible for everything! Not just the care of my children, but their education, as well. No thanks! I had several reasons...excuses honestly...but no thanks!

The day I took Danielle in to register for third grade, she cried. "I thought you were going to homeschool us," she pleaded.

My heart broke and my defenses dropped. God used Danielle's words and tears to open my heart, to stop me and make me think. And so, we began. I ordered books and we started the school year as new homeschoolers. I'm so glad that I did. It was the best decision for both kids.

Devin was a bright child. He could read and write well by this time. If we had read him a story once, he could recite it back to us. Math, writing, memorizing, it didn't matter, he could do it. Sitting still was a different story. Man, he was a busy kid! ADD, ADHD or busy boy, he would've been labeled in a standard classroom. Instead of being sorted out and labeled, here at home he did academic work in the mornings with me and ran outside the rest of the day. He worked with Curt and drove every piece of machinery. That kid can actually visualize any page he has read. He is better than any APP at finding Bible verses.

Devin was too bright for our school system. He would have been bored, or he would have caused trouble. When Devin was 18 or so and away at a college, he called one day to tell me he was glad we had homeschooled, and that I shouldn't even consider putting the younger 3 in public school…EVER! I love that kid.

I am ever so grateful that God kept pushing, showing me that I needed to homeschool, that I could, and that the kids would do well. Homeschooling gave us the chance to do many things. We sewed quilts and baked. We grew crystals, raised snails and created science experiments. And, yes, we did academics, too. I wouldn't change that decision. I have no regrets!

It may not be homeschooling for you. It may be something else but be open to where God is leading you. He wants the very best for you.

Mommy, you got this!!

Mommy Moment…

It was spring. Dani was six. She wanted to dress up for something at school but didn't want her shoes to get muddy walking up our muddy driveway. She decided to wear her black irrigation boots over her shoes. She came home in tears! The older kids on the bus had teased her. My heart broke.

I had been terribly teased as a child. This moment brought up all those years, all those tears, and all that pain.

I comforted her. I struggled not to make her pain my own. I desperately wanted to keep her from the kind of pain I had suffered. We talked about those kids' hearts. I told her that they hurt her, because they hurt. In the end we decided that Dani would not wear those boots again. If necessary, I'd drive her up the driveway, so her shoes would not get muddy.

When she started out the door the next day to meet the bus, I looked down. There she stood in her black boots. I was overwhelmed with emotion.

"Dolly, you don't have to wear those. I will take you!"

"Mommy, it's THEIR problem." She turned and started out the door.

In this moment I had a choice. I could dump my past on my baby girl, or I could leave it at the foot of the cross. My past made me who I am. I can't change my past. God protected me in so many ways. I am oh so grateful for His care.

That choice came up several times as our kids were growing. Satan loves to attack where you have a weakness. This day I hugged her, kissed her, sent her on her way, and sat down and cried. I prayed desperately for God to protect her from those kids. I prayed for her to be strong. I cried some more.

No one tells you how hard it is to be a mom. There is no training, other than on the job training.

I have learned that the Creator of all, loves my kids even more than I do. If I will turn to Him in prayer, trust Him, and listen to Him. He will guide me and help me.

I know He loves you and your children as well.

Mommy, you got this!!

Mommy Moment...

When I started dating Curt, I really was a "city girl." I hadn't ever been on a working farm, never driven a tractor, never used a shovel. Most of our dates revolved around him irrigating his fields. He didn't have those big sprinklers that you see. He had a three-foot-wide open ditch that ran along the top of each field and aluminum tubes that worked like straws to carry the water from the ditch into the rows in the field.

One night when we stopped to move the tubes to different rows, we found that the ditch had washed out, and water was rushing out into the field. Curt quickly assessed the situation and told me he would have to "set a canvas".

I thought he was speaking in some foreign language or making up things. A canvas is something you paint, not set in muddy water.

Then he hands ME a shovel and tells ME to fill in the break while he goes to shut off the water.

Again, with the foreign language!

There I was in the dark all alone with this shovel. Water is POURING out of the ditch washing out the rows of corn. I'm shoveling, but it's washing the new dirt away faster than I can fill it in. I don't know what to do! I don't want to disappoint Curt. I can't shovel any faster. I'm not strong enough to scoop more dirt on the shovel.

What could I do?!

Panic. I panicked!

Then I had a thought... I sat in it.

It worked, don't laugh.

Curt laughed PLENTY when he returned to find his date sitting in the ditch, covered in mud, eyes wide begging for approval.

Sometimes you just gotta do what ya gotta do! It might not be pretty, but you just do it anyway. Motherhood is a lot like that. You know you have to do something, but you aren't sure what. God helped me through it. I am sure He will help you as well.

Mommy, you got this!!

Mommy Moment...

At about a year littles like to pull themselves up to the dishwasher door and stand there throwing the silverware out. Soon they love to grab the broom the second you set it against the wall, spinning around with it, knocking things down. By two, that fresh laundry that you have just gotten out of the dryer and set on the couch to fold is fair game for flinging all over the house.

How can you get anything done? Most mommies get aggravated at the child. Some have resorted to cleaning the house when the kids are asleep or not at home.

What if there was another way? What if you could put their interest and energy to good use?

As I said before, my littles were in the kitchen with me all the time. I had a drawer full of little toys that they were allowed, and encouraged, to play with. That's true. But if I was loading the dishwasher and 10-month-old Jenna was standing there, I'd hand her each spoon. At first, I had to show her how to slide them into the slot. Soon she could do it without prompting.

When sweeping, I'd get out the little handheld broom for them. I could sweep the kitchen and they "swept" their little area.

Laundry can be a trick. Having a 2-year-old fold sheets or jeans probably won't work. What if you set a pile of clean washrags and kitchen towels out for them to fold and you do the rest?

Littles LOVE to help! I know they aren't really any help, but they can be taught bit by bit. Letting her put the spoons in the dishwasher may seem pointless, but I would beg to differ. I think it IS the point. Teaching them to do…and enjoy… simple tasks prepare them to do harder tasks and to enjoy working with you. It may feel silly to hand the small broom to a 2-year-old but show them how to use it and soon they will clean up after themselves.

Mommy, you aren't the maid. You are the mother, teacher, and trainer. I've read, "Train up a child in the way he should go…" I took that to mean exactly what it said. Training starts at birth, one bit at a time you get to train them how to be an adult.

Everyday there are so many teaching moments! Time is so fleeting… trust me on that. Use the time that you have, start each day on purpose. LOVE the time you are allowed.

Mommy, you got this!!

Mommy Moment...

Jenna needed a bit of special care, which meant we had quite a bill when all was said and done. Actually, we owed a year's wage to the hospital for her care. Mind you, that was only $10,000, but that truly was a year's wage for us. We ran a super tight budget, and this seemed impossible to pay off. I met with the accounts clerk and set up payments. $200 per month is what they told me we would have to pay. It seemed an impossibility.

We scraped together every extra penny we could each month. Then we'd pray.

It never seemed like we would have enough, but each month we made our payment somehow.

We had been at this for about a year. One day I walked into the hospital to make a payment. The nice lady accepted my check, pulled up our account and turned back to me. "I see this is your last payment," she said pleasantly.

I'm sure I responded. I have no memory of the exact words I said. I remember smiling, thanking her and walking out.

I got to my car somehow. I sat in it and cried. I may not be the best at math, but $200 per month for twelve or thirteen months doesn't add up to $10,000.

God had taken care of it. Someway, somehow He had paid this bill. I don't know why He did, but I know He did, and I am grateful.

Turn to Him. Trust him. Walk with Him and He will do great things!!

Mommy, you got this!!

Mommy Moment...

The night before I was to pick up our daughter, son-in-law and baby grandson, I was awake praying about the baby's sleeping arrangements. I have a port-a-crib, but it's difficult for Jenna to lay a babe down into.

They were coming to celebrate Christmas a bit late. Jenna and baby Declan were to stay for several days. They needed a place to be while Colton was on a 3-week temporary duty for the Air-force.

When she had come for a short visit the month before, Declan woke up nearly every time she tried to transfer him into that bed. She ended up with him in her bed with her most nights. Neither of them slept well that way. I pondered the problem, prayed for an answer and went on to sleep.

I had to leave right after breakfast to get to DIA to get them. On my drive, again I prayed. I made up my mind that if Jen felt he slept better in a regular crib I would buy a mattress on our way home, and we would repurpose an old, wooden twin frame into a crib for him. It wouldn't be pretty, but it would work.

Their flight landed. I met them with no trouble. We were traveling along visiting about her stay. I asked her about the bed. After a bit of discussion, we decided, yes, it would be best for baby to have a new bed. We planned to stop for the mattress.

All settled.

Nope. God had a better plan.

Not 15 minutes later, a friend of ours texted and offered to give us a mini crib!! She knew nothing of our dilemma or our decision.

It gets better... The crib is actually painted green. Jenna's favorite color!! You may think it's just a coincidence. Not me. I know it was an answer to prayer.

Sweet Mommy, cast your cares on Him. He doesn't always say yes or answer so very quickly, but He always answers. Look to Him. Trust Him. He loves you all!

Mommy, you got this!!

Mommy Moment...

God has used each of my little ones to teach me so very much...He still does.

Devin was the one used to teach me to talk to people. I had become extremely shy in public settings. He had a love for people. He wanted to talk to them, even though his vocabulary was limited. He was curious about them. He would talk to EVERYONE. His sweet little smile made all the ladies in the stores stop and talk to him...well, usually.

I'd be pushing the cart, Danielle standing on the front, and Devin in the cart seat. We'd be happily filling the cart with needed items. Every time we'd pass a person, Devin would smile big. Of course, they'd smile back. Sometimes they'd start up a conversation with him. But, if for some reason they didn't talk with him, he'd turn to them and ask in his sweet 2-year-old voice, "What's yous name?" If he got no answer, he'd ask again...a little bit louder. If they still didn't answer, he'd turn to me and state QUITE loudly, "Day don't tell me yous name."

If I could've melted right there in the store, I would have.

I couldn't, so I didn't. I actually began to enjoy watching people's reactions. I knew his innocent heart could disarm most folks. Generally, people responded nicely. -Thankfully.

When he first began to do this, I tried to 'hush' him, but very soon I understood that people were important to him. I had to get over myself. I let him be who God created him to be.

He is still that sweet, friendly little boy whom people like to talk to.

Mommy, God made them individually. Each child is different. Look for the heart behind the behavior. Devin wasn't meaning to be rude. He simply cared about the folks in the store. He meant no harm. I just needed the wisdom to see his heart. God will give you wisdom to see the hearts of your children.

I promise. Just ask Him.

Mommy, you got this!!

Mommy Moment...

After naps Danielle, Devin and I walked down to the farmyard to see Curt. It was a lovely day for a walk. We skipped, sang songs and soaked up some sunshine. We found Curt working in the shed. We are a bit of a distraction, so we didn't stay long, and I had to get back home to get ready to go into town. We gathered the eggs from the chicken house before we left the farmyard. The kids loved "hunting eggs."

Walking back home was always slow. Its 1/2 mile and their 4 and 2-year-old legs were short.

Once home I set the egg bucket on the table, told Danielle I was going to take a quick shower. I'd be right back, just play with Devin for a bit. Off I went.

There I was, in the shower, when Danielle comes rushing in… terribly distraught. I knew something awful had happened. Her words were all jumbled together. I grab a towel, throw it around me and dash out, dripping water everywhere, to see what has happened to Devin.

I have an overactive imagination, so I was braced for anything...except the truth. THAT turned out to be quite surprising.

I got to the kitchen, and there sat Devin, happy as a lark, grinning from ear to ear...ON the table. Smack dab in the middle with the once full egg bucket between his legs. I spotted him just in time to see what made him so happy.

He was throwing the eggs on the floor and laughing as they SPLATTED on the floor.

He was so very happy. It was so very funny....and so ***very*** messy.

Sometime joy comes in the unexpected.

Mommy, you got this!!

Mommy Moment...

I had never been around a milk cow before. Curt raised beef cattle and then Holsteins (big black and white dairy cows), but he didn't milk them. So we knew nothing when we purchased a jersey from one of

Jenna's friends. We named her Honey because our animals tend to live up to their names and we needed her to be sweet.

Jenna and I read up on hand milking before Honey delivered her calf. Curt got us a milk bucket; made us a stanchion (a place to feed and milk her simultaneously) and we were ready. Although there had been quite the learning curve, we felt like we were doing pretty well. Oh, we did have a few mornings when she would tip over the bucket or wouldn't stand still, but overall, we were successful at milking our cow.

All the experts in all the books I had read said cows needed milked at regular intervals. If you were going to milk 3 times per day, then you milk every 8 hours. If you were only milking twice a day, then it should be every 12 hours. 6:00am and 6:00pm worked brilliantly for us all summer and into fall.

I went out one Sunday morning. Honey was lying right outside of her stanchion. The sun wasn't up yet, so I had to be a bit careful walking across to her. As you know, I'm not the most coordinated. I spoke to her and she looked at me. She didn't get up. That's a bit odd, I thought. She was highly food motivated and we fed her while we milked her. I kept talking to her and she just laid there. I sat the bucket down, opened the stanchion gate and she still just laid there. I started to panic.

"Get up! You must get up. Is something wrong? Are you sick? You can't be sick! You just can't be!"

She just laid there.

I began to pray, asking God for wisdom, trying not to cry.

"Come on, Honey. You have to get up! I have to milk you!!" I poked and prodded. I pushed her I pulled her. No luck. I tried a bit of grain. No luck. I actually sat on her bouncing a bit, trying to get her up. I ran back up to the house. Crying all the way.

Frantically I told Curt what had happened and asked him what to do. He is always the calm to my panic. Go try again was what we decided, and then we'd have to call a vet.

All my fussing about had taken about an hour. The sun was up by the time I went back down to her.

There she stood...waiting on ME! Giving me such a look! She didn't know about Daylight Savings time. She only knew the sun hadn't been up and it was now.

That day I learned that both of us were city girls at heart, me and my cow.

Mommy, you got this!!

Mommy Moment...

You already know I was a clueless young mommy, married at 18, our first baby before my 19th birthday. I was a dedicated mommy, a delighted mommy, too. I adored my husband and my little girl. I learned so much that first year. I learned how to bathe a baby, and not cry; How to let her sleep in her own bed; and not cry; How to cook, and not cry. Also, on the list, don't over feed her, she will puke if you do, and you will cry.

I was standing in our kitchen one day holding her when it hit me. I was a mother. It sounds ridiculous. I was OBVIOUSLY a mother. What hit me that day was that I was totally responsible for this baby girl. Me? I knew nothing about being a good mother. Everything that happened to her was my responsibility. Her physical safety and growth, her mental development, her social skills and manners, her spiritual teaching, the nutrition she got...all up to me? Whose idea was this? I wasn't capable!

I began to cry. I began to pray. I knew of God but had not truly chosen to trust or follow Him. That day I made a choice. I would follow and trust Him. If God had entrusted her to me, surely, He would help me raise her.

I can honestly say I was clueless, but God led me each step of the way. I began listening to Dr. Dobson's radio program. I read the books he recommended. I read the Bible, searching for parenting advice. Turns out it's full of great advice!

I made a ton of mistakes! I let my emotions get the best of me more often than they should have. I slacked off at times and didn't really parent. Yet, God was there each time I turned to Him.

I'd encourage you to define the word "parent." What does it mean to parent? What type of parent do you want your kids to have? No one is perfect. Give yourself some grace but take your responsibility seriously. Intentionally train your kids, spend time with them and teach them. Most of all enjoy them. They are only little once. Mine are all grown up. I can honestly say I love who they are as adults. And yet, I miss those busy, messy, wild days.

Mommy, you got this!!

Mommy Moment...

My mom was not the typical grandmother. She didn't spoil the kids in the normal "give the child everything it wants and send it home" way. She DID things with her grandchildren. She played cards. She went on daytrips. She went on vacation. Mom even took line dancing lessons with Danielle when she was 72! She was awesome.

Devin was 8 when Curt gave him his first motorcycle. It was a birthday present. Devin was so thrilled!! He rode around and around in our yard. Mom was here that day. He was showing her how well he could drive, and he offered to give her a ride.

Well, of course Mom was more than willing! I had my reservations. After all, he was only eight and it was new to him. He wasn't exactly an experienced driver.

He was a smart little guy. He understood that the additional weight would require more power. She confidently got on behind him. I closed my eyes. He gave it a little extra gas and popped the clutch.

It did a bit of a wheelie. Mom slid back. Devin drove off. And there lay my mom...on the ground, in the middle of our driveway...laughing!

Don't miss the moments that matter to their hearts. Mom understood that. She knew just how important it was to Devin's little heart that she trusted him. She knew the risk but put his heart above her concern. I didn't always get that, but she did.

There is no reason to take yourself so seriously that you miss the moments that are truly important to them. Kids need you to be all in.

Mommy, you got this!!

Mommy Moment...

Have you noticed that little people see things differently than adults?

Sundays in our home always involved going to church. We had quite a routine. If we were going to make it on time to church, showers or baths had to be taken Saturday night. The girls' hair had to be braided or put up then, or it would never be done before church. Chores had to be done; animals needed to be fed first thing Sunday morning. Breakfast had to be on time. Lunch had to be started. And of course, everyone had to get dressed and do so in time to make it to church. I usually rushed around in a bit of a frenzy trying to insure everyone was ready.

I was running late. I was out of the shower and hurriedly dressing for church when Devin came walking into the room. He looked so cute in his suit pants and little dress shirt! He must have been 4 at the time. "Mommy, can you put my belt on me?"

Nearly every week he asked me this same question. He couldn't get his belt through the belt loops once he had his pants on. Why didn't he put the belt through the loops before he put them on? That was a great question, one I had asked many times. I was so exasperated!

I knelt down to him, took the belt and put it through the loops... again. "Sweetie, what will you do when I'm not around to put your belt on you?"

He looked up sweetly and replied, "My arms will be longer then."

Who could argue with that sweet, earnest answer? He was so right. I look back and think he just needed affirmation that I was there and that I would always help him, even if I was in a hurry.

Keep your eyes open for insights into their hearts.

Mommy, you got this!!

Mommy Moment...

Our family has a gap in it. We had the typical American family with the average number of kids, two. They were 2 1/2 years apart. Perfect, right? Then God started working on my heart. So, years went by with our perfect family, and then I got pregnant. I was only pregnant for a couple months before I lost the baby. Six months later, the same story. I lost several babies in the first trimester. I have since learned that it is typical when you have taken birth control. Apparently, The Pill depletes the body of its vitamin B. Without that essential vitamin, you have a difficult time keeping a pregnancy.

I also miscarried 3 different times in the second trimester before I became pregnant with Jenna. I had gotten to the point that I just didn't tell anyone that I was pregnant. Curt of course knew, but we didn't say anything to anyone else. As a matter of fact, I was 6 1/2 months along with Jen before I told my mom. I had only told her because at that point she asked if I was expecting.

The last miscarriage was the most difficult. I hadn't been to the Doctor. What was the point if I was just going to miscarry again? I was 5 1/2 months along. I had been feeling fine and actually was ready to tell Mom I was expecting. Curt was working in our garage that day, changing oil in the car or something. The kids were happily playing in the yard. Without going into detail, let's just use a farm term and say I sluffed the baby. I felt weak and lightheaded. Thirty minutes passed. I was still weak and lightheaded, and knew I needed to tell Curt what had happened. I knew I would need him to check in on me every few minutes. If the feeling of light headedness didn't go away, I was going to pass out soon.

I did manage to get to the garage door. What I said to Curt in a weak and weary voice was something like, "Check on me in a few minutes. I may need to go to the hospital." I shut the door. Walked back into our bedroom and laid on the bed, hoping my body would recover.

Poor guy! I scared him to death! He came running right in to find me. I was fine. I rested for the rest of the day and did recover.

I tell you that because I need you all to know that I do understand the pain of loss. I tell funny stories from the events from our past, but those don't tell the whole story. Day to day we were, and are, a happy family. We have been so very blessed!! But... I understand that some of you hurt. I know that in this world our lives aren't always what we had hoped they would be.

The miscarriages were a part of the years I call "The Hard Years." We had lots of junk going on, Medical debt, cancer scare, Dad's death, and a dozen other things. Those years were awful! At times, all I could see was the awful stuff. I struggled to see the beauty and goodness that was all around me. I wrote before that I struggled with depression. I know some of you are struggling now.

I need you to see that there is hope! You will make it through the rough stuff. I did. We have so many blessings now! The hard years were just a small part of our story. Your hard years will also be a small part of YOUR story. They are horrible to go through, but they do pass. Your joy will be made new. I have a sign that reads, "Let your light shine so that others can see their way out of the darkness." I pray that my little light will help you see your way out.

Mommy, you got this!!

Mommy moment...

We have seen many miracles in our 37 years together. One such miracle happened when Caleb was young, maybe 8. It was a warm fall day. As usual, he was happily playing outside. Lunch was nearly ready, the table was set, and Curt was on his way.

Caleb came running in the back door. He had been stung on the chin by a wasp. His chin was swollen. His glands were beginning to swell also.

I tried to remain calm, talking sweetly to him to keep him calm. I gave him some Benadryl. Called the doctor. By the time we got to the Dr's office the swelling was decreasing. After checking Caleb and writing a prescription for an EpiPen he looked me in the eye, WITH Caleb right there, and said, "Next time he gets stung he will either have no reaction whatsoever, or his reaction will worsen. If that happens there probably won't be time to do much of anything."

He actually said there was really no reason to fill the prescription because, unless Caleb kept it with him at ALL times there wouldn't be time to use it. How frightening!

I talked to Caleb about it on the way home and hoped he wasn't too traumatized. He acted just fine. I prayed it would never happen again.

I prayed and pondered. Every day was a struggle not to fall into fear. Losing Caleb would've been devastating for our family. Time went by and it became easier to believe it would be fine. That thought was tested a year or so later.

Caleb came to the back door and said he'd been stung. He was acting brave because we had a little neighbor girl with us, and he didn't want to frighten her. My heart failed me. I could hardly breathe. But there he stood looking into my eyes. I got my act together, took hold of his hand, and sat right down on the floor with him in my lap.

My mind was playing the words of the Dr. over and over. My heart was begging God to let him live and my mouth was singing gently to my sweet trusting son. My eyes were welling up with tears. At first, the tears were there because, in 5 to 10 minutes I'd know his body's reaction, and I was afraid. After singing a few songs, they were grateful tears pouring down my cheeks, because he was still alive.

God let us keep Caleb that day. We are ever so grateful for this miracle.

We dedicated each child to God at their birth. We prayed daily for God to watch over them. We understood that they were God's children before they were ours. We are stewards of these precious gifts. We hold them only temporarily. Seeing children as gifts from God and yourself as a steward will change the way you parent.

Mommy, you got this!!

Mommy Moment...

We were working cattle with our neighbors. Six or seven guys were running them through the working chute, giving shots, and checking for horns. I was no help, but I was there with Dani and Devin. Dani was old enough to stand on the bench on the outside of the chute. Devin was a babe in my arms. They loved 'working' with Dad.

I hadn't thought about what the kids might hear or see. Out of the blue, Dani suddenly shouted all the words that she had heard the men say. I was dumbstruck!! They weren't words we NEVER said. Yet, she just put them ALL in a sentence perfectly mimicking the men's vocabulary.

What do you do? I grew up hearing those words, but they were SHOCKING from my four-year-old.

The words we use matter. The Bible says they bring life or death. Our words come from our hearts and play over in our OWN heads. We all have words that play in our heads, "you're not good enough", "you never do anything right", or if we are lucky, "you can do it' and "you are so loved". I'd encourage you to think about the words you use. Are they words that bring life to your kids? Are they encouraging to their hearts?

I ignored those words that day. She never said any of them again, and I am so glad. The situation served to teach me that kids hear EVERYTHING! Be intentional with every word you say.

Mommy, you got this!!

Mommy Moment...

If faith in God is important to you, it can be challenging to help your littles have their OWN faith. It's easy for them to just go through the motions of faith without ever trusting for themselves. It has been an important part of my parenting to help our kids have their own belief in Christ.

We prayed as a family over all our meals. (I often joke that we pray because I'm the cook) The kids prayed at night with either Curt or me. We attended church, so again they were involved in prayer. Praying was taken seriously; we made sure to teach respectfulness, just not legalism. We didn't correct prayers; we just let them say what they wanted to say. It may have been silly or childish, but it was their prayer. We felt God was big enough to sort it out. We just wanted them to feel like they could talk to God about anything and everything, good or bad.

Jen was probably 3 when she started praying the same words for every prayer. Lunch time, bedtime, in Sunday School, it didn't matter. It was always the same. I so wish she could have communicated where they came from or what they really meant. I asked around at church and no one used the phrase. We never learned the origin or true meaning. Her words were the always the same. She went months saying, "And I say to the day of the Lord. Amen."

That was it, nothing more.

It made us chuckle, but she was intensely serious. One day we may learn the meaning, or we may never know. It's ok either way. God knows and He heard that sweet, faith filled prayer of that tiny little girl.

He hears your prayers, too. Turn to Him and trust Him to sort out the details.

Mommy, you got this!!

Mommy Moment...

I had a cyst growing in my neck. It had happened twice before, both times ending in surgery. This time, I accidentally saw the doctor's note in the chart that said it was likely cancerous. I was so frightened. Not for me, but for my kids. I had been praying. Well, I was begging honestly. The weird thing is… I had an odd feeling that I just couldn't shake. It was this feeling that God had a bigger purpose, and I should trust Him. That's easier said than done.

Let me add right here, that every time I had gotten in my car to go to an appointment one particular song was on. EVERY TIME. Every time I turned on the radio in the house, the same song played. EVERY

TIME. At first, I though "Wow. This song is popular." Then I began to listen to the words and notice just how often it was on. "You lift me up" by Selah was the song. It reminded me that God was in control and He was holding on to me. It calmed my heart each time it played.

Following one Dr appointment I attended our local homeschool meeting. The ladies prayed and asked me to let them know what day the surgery would be. Sure, I could do that. I'd send an email as soon as I heard. I did as I'd promised, but I added an unusual line, a phrase I never use. I've certainly, never sent it out in any email, before or since. "My surgery is scheduled for Wednesday (whatever date*) unless God heals me.*"

Wow! A bit presumptuous! I actually typed it in jest…or so I thought.

The Friday before my scheduled surgery on Wednesday, I imagined the visible lump was gone. Surely, I was imagining things. I have a wild imagination. I know I do. So, I determined not to look again. Odd, I know. I truly refused to look in a mirror for the next 2 days. I just closed my eyes as I went by the mirror and prayed. Actually, I just prayed no matter where I was. I'm sure I was a terribly distracted mother for those days. Finally, Sunday night I asked Curt to look at my neck. I don't believe I told him why. He verified my imaginings. It wasn't there!

It's amazing how quickly a doctor can clear a spot in his schedule when you call to cancel surgery!

He walked into the small examination room all snarky. "I hear you think your cyst is gone like…magic."

"No. Like…MIRACLE!"

He checked for the cyst. Then He canceled my surgery.

The story wasn't over yet. Klove radio station called just a few weeks later. I was randomly chosen as the winner of 2 concert tickets they were giving away. Guess which concert they were for…Selah!

I was so overwhelmed! I had NOT entered that contest. So many tears were cried. God doesn't always act in such a dramatic way in my life. I have no idea why He chose to act in this way in that situation. I simply know, He did, and I'm grateful! His word says to trust Him and pray!

Mommy, you got this!!

Mommy Moment…

Mom, Dad and I moved from Denver after I finished 2nd grade. My siblings all stayed in Denver. They had their own lives. My grandfather had died, and Grandma wasn't all that well. It was a tough move for Mom. She left a home she loved, her friends, three of her kids, all to take care of her mother who had been abusive to her. It took Mom years to really get over the move. She functioned. She did all the things a mommy should, but she wasn't happy. When my siblings would come for a visit, she was a whole different person. She became her old self. She was happy. She would cook real meals. I hated when they would leave. I remember times when they were loading up their cars and calling my name, so I could say goodbye to them. I didn't answer. I couldn't. I was hiding behind the house crying. It was miserable. Mom was only happy when they were there. I didn't want them to leave. After Grandma passed away and we moved to another small town, Brush, and life got better for her.

As a little girl in all of that, I kind of became my own parent. Dad worked. Mom worked. I was on my own a lot. When My brother and his wife started building a home, Mom and Dad wanted to help them.

I went along with them at first. I must have become a problem, so it wasn't long before they would leave me home when they went to help. That meant I was alone for weekends...at nine or ten years old.

I remember the first time it happened. I was to spend the weekend with a neighbor. Mom had it all set up. She helped me pack my little suitcase. I was to walk over when they left. Well...I did walk over. I walked up their front steps. I knocked on their door. When the neighbor lady opened it, I calmly explained that my mother had changed her mind. I would not need to spend the weekend with them. I marched down the steps and straight back home. Where I stayed till my folks returned.

Can you imagine!! I have no idea what my poor mother thought when the neighbor talked to her. I only remember not having to go over there, or anywhere else, when Mom and Dad were gone.

I was good. I mean, I felt safe at home, me, the dog, the cat and God. What else did I need? That neighbor scared me. I had deemed them "creepy people" in my wise and discerning little mind. I felt safer at home all alone.

Mommy, you got this!!

Mommy moment...

When Jenna was a toddler, we discovered several of her molars were deteriorating. The dentist thought it was because of the challenges immediately following her birth. We found a dentist that specialized in children's care and began periodic visits. That first visit was brutal! She was so frightened of the x-ray machine. I ended up holding her down in hopes of calming her. I think I made it worse. I was heartbroken and crying. What a mess!! Anyhow, we spent thousands of dollars on dental work…money we didn't have to spend. Our accounts were mostly empty. I was praying and crying…

Yes. I cried a LOT when I was a young mom. More than I probably should have. It was all so hard for me.

… We had no idea how we were going to pay those bills. Out of the blue we got a check in the mail one day. An older couple who had been friends of Curt's family had both passed away and left a bit of money to Curt's cousins, siblings and him. They had no children of their own. By the time it was divided up it wasn't a huge amount, but nearly exactly what we needed to pay our bill at the dentist. I have never been so grateful to someone I didn't know.

Jenna still remembers the first visit, as do I, but she also remembers liking to go to the dentist. It didn't permanently scar her. I'm not so sure about me, I still feel traumatized by that first visit.

God used this experience to strengthen my resolve to trust in Him. It's one of those moments of provision, which proved to me that He would take care of us. Yes, we had to be faithful and diligent, but He was with us. He was walking beside us. He will walk with you as well. Turn to Him, take all your emotions and challenges to Him. He is FAITHFUL.

Mommy, you got this!!

Mommy Moment…

Recently I learned that the game two of our girls started when they were about six and eight years old is still going on. They are twenty-four and twenty-six!! That is a long time to play one game.

Want to know what game they are playing?

I must go back to the beginning. Our younger three did all kinds of crafts. They made potholders. They sewed pillows and quilts. They made jewelry. They created bead animals. You get the idea. Well, they not only made those items, but they sold them. At some point the two girls created a bead lizard in black and white beads. They aptly named it Skunk.

Skunk didn't get sold. He became the "traveling" lizard. He was the main character in their game. They started hiding Skunk in odd places for Dad to find. One day Skunk might be in Curt's boot. A few days later Jenna might find Skunk above her mirror. Curt might find Skunk on his scroll saw next week. As time progressed and the girls became older, Skunk might be found on a car visor or in a coffee cup.

You get the idea. Skunk was hidden and found and re-hidden ALL OVER THE HOUSE!

I think they even lost him once and remade a Skunk so the game would continue.

Last week during Jenna's visit, Skunk made another appearance. The three of them have been hiding this silly bead lizard once again. It's a bit of a shock to pour out what you think will be your vitamin and find yourself holding a black and white lizard!!!!!

I LOVE IT!!!!! I don't play. It is their game. I just watch. Isn't it awesome to watch your kids enjoy their relationship with their dad?

I think the same is true as a Christian mom when your children have their own relationship with God. It is a joyous thing to sit back and just watch them relate to God, to walk with Him and have joy in that relationship.

Mommy, you got this!!

Mommy Moment...

Because of the age gap in our family there were only a few years when all five were in the house, Danielle is about 15 years older than Caleb. Those years brought a jumble of emotions and were a bit of a scheduling nightmare. Danielle was learning to drive while Caleb was learning to walk. Jenna and Kali were playing with dolls while Devin was a competitive marksman. It was tough to keep up with them all. But I loved it. We had bad days like every family does, but it was fun to watch the older two interact with the younger three.

We have a photo of Devin giving Caleb a ride on his motorcycle. The look of pride and exhilaration on both of their faces says it all. Devin is thrilled to have his baby brother with him, and Caleb is feeling like such a big kid with his big brother!

People ask if it was hard to have 5 kids. Parenting is hard no matter how many you have. It takes a lot of faith and determination to run a household whether you have ten kids or two.

My mother-in-law always told me, once you have three you get over yourself. I think, she was right. I got over myself and trusted God more. But we didn't stop at three…THANK THE LORD. We would have missed out on so much joy if we had.

Your life may be hard, Sweet Mommy, but everyone has challenges. Find a mentor or someone to help you through the tough days. Learn from your mistakes. Look for even just one moment of joy in each day.

Mommy, you got this!!

Mommy Moment...

You may wonder what a day with us and our five might have been like. I will attempt to give you a glimpse.

Breakfast was at 6 am. We had to be up and moving early since we farmed. Curt was out irrigating by 5:30 and returned in time to eat with us. All the kids helped prepare all the meals. They didn't always cook, but they set the table, swept the floor, and did dishes. They all took turns cooking and certainly knew how. We rotated the chores, so that they all learned to do each job. Once breakfast was finished, we began school. Academic work was done in the morning from 7:00 until 11:00 am. Then we fixed lunch. Curt came back to the house at noon. He usually took the youngest ones in to lay down for naps after we ate lunch. Afternoons were more complicated, piano practices, piano lessons, helping on the farm, crafts, baking, or sports practices. It all depended on the year. Evenings were quiet. Supper was at 6:00, after which we did dishes and cleaned up the kitchen, the kids read and played around till 7:30 littles were put to bed at that time. Curt would gather the kids around him, and they'd read a bedtime story, two if they could talk Daddy into it. Then he'd chase them off to bed. I mean that literally. He would chase them around. They'd squeal! Oh, how they loved bedtime routine!! I'd kiss and tuck them in. Then Daddy would pray with them each.

Silence at last

Simple? Yes. Easy? Not always. I am such a...ummm...non perfectionist?... free spirit? Curt provided the framework of our schedule. I needed the routine. Funny thing, the kids needed it, too. We all knew what to expect each day. It gave us all security. It was the framework for our days.

As parents we often want to give more, do more. We often forget kids like routine. They thrive in the mundane and ordinary.

Mommy, you got this!!

Mommy Moment...

You'd think after being on the farm for 20+ years, and raising baby animals and kids that whole time, that I'd have acquired some sense. Not so, apparently.

I told you Jenna and I had a milk cow, Honey. We had lambs and goats well before that. Curt had always brought up any bum lambs from the farm that had little to no chance of survival for me to try to save and then I could raise them.

If they lived. I so miss them. A sweet friend gave Jenna a baby goat for her 10th birthday. We were used to farm animals, so it was a great gift. She loved that goat. She had been with us for years by the time we got our milk cow.

We had been milking our cow quite successfully all summer. In October of that first year we were milking Honey, I was cleaning out the garden. In the past, I had fed all the leftover vegetation to the goat. She just loved all the vines and dead vegetation. She was a great way to dispose of all of it. She would wait by the fence dancing around and talking to me. We had done that for the five years we had her. But...we had NOT had a milk cow during those years.

The goat was so excited to see me come to the fence with the leftovers from the garden! Honey was out in the pasture and wasn't even aware of what I was doing. I threw all of it over the fence, talked to the goat for a moment and went back to work.

Those garden leftovers included some onions. Do you have any idea what happens to a cow's milk when you feed her ONIONS??! Yep. It tastes like onions. Actually, for 3 days it tastes like onions. Not a good flavor for milk.

There are only a few recipes you can make with onion-milk, scalloped potatoes, potato soup, clam chowder. Ummm...that's about it.

I have read "Anne of Green Gables" and totally understand her frustration with 'getting into scrapes. 'When will I finally outgrow childish scrapes?

Mommy, you got this!!

Mommy Moment...

Over the past 25 years we have hosted over 40 foreign students in our home. Some stayed six months, some just a weekend, most were with us for three weeks. We've hosted through a couple of programs. Our favorite program is the 4H IFYE program. The kids are mostly college age and have some interest in Agriculture so it's a good fit. When you host that many people you end up with dear friends all over the world …and a whole lot of funny memories.

The kids had the breakfast table set and I was just setting the biscuits on when our guest came out of his room to join us. We all smiled at him and said good morning. He took one look at breakfast and left!

He went right back into his room!

The kids were confused. We were all puzzled by his behavior. Had we offended him somehow? Was there something wrong with the food?

He returned a few minutes later with his camera and proceeded to photograph our breakfast!

"Is this normal?! " "Do you eat this often?" "Do restaurants serve this?" "I mean, can I order this at restaurants?" "Like, at a REAL restaurant?" He was full of questions about our food. We answered politely, but with every question we were more confused.

What were we having, you may wonder? It was biscuits and sausage gravy. It's a perfectly normal food to us., but a perfectly STRANGE food to him.

Don't worry. He was a lovely guest and we quite enjoyed our time with him. And he learned to love biscuits and sausage gravy.

Mommy, you got this!!

Mommy Moment...

My kids were quite young when I began to pray for their future spouses. I prayed for God to guide them to the person, He wanted them to marry.

Danielle and Devin had tied at their last 4-H muzzleloader competition. It was so much fun to watch them shoot together. Devin is nearly 3 years younger, but he had the goal of beating her score. He matched her, shot for shot, all day. They won the State match and earned the right to go to nationals! A proud mommy moment.

The National competition is a big deal. Kids from across the country come and compete in archery, .22, pistol, and muzzleloader. Since Danielle was on the team, they needed a female chaperone. That's me.

You know, it was the first time in 19 years I felt like I didn't have to "mommy" any one or be the responsible one. Actually, the first time EVER.

We had a BLAST! Our coach knew another coach, so the two teams hung out together in our free time. We went to dinner together the first night so the kids could get to know each other. I, being a bit bored, blew my straw paper at Danielle just as Coach was explaining that the kids should be on their best behavior. Oops. And, at our picnic the next day, the kids and I were having a squirt gun fight all around our cabin area. Someone, who shall remain nameless, was even diving in and out of the windows. Then, we had a watermelon seed spitting fight, and spit seeds at each other. It was GREAT fun!

The best part…besides taking 3rd as a team…was the drive home. Danielle was trying to help me stay awake. It was 1 or 2 in the morning. We were visiting about our trip. I asked her about the guys there. Was there anyone whom she might be interested in? "No!!" Came a quick answer. "They are all immature." Long pause…

"Well. All except that one guy Jeff. He reminds me of Dad."

I warned Curt that if a guy named Jeff ever calls, we were in trouble.

And the rest, shall we say, is history! They were married a year and a half later.

Mommy, you got this!!

Mommy Moment...

I have led you to believe that Danielle was a perfect child. Au contraire!

I was happily cleaning the house one Saturday morning. Danielle was "helping". We had swept the kitchen. We had folded the load of laundry. Now we were cleaning the bathroom. When it was finished, I realized the Kleenex box was empty, so I replaced it. I pulled that first Kleenex up a bit and headed off to work in the kitchen. Soon I hear a happy little squeal from the bathroom.

What do you think I found in there?

There sat that sweet little 18-month-old sitting on the bathroom floor with a huge grin surrounded by every pink Kleenex that had been in that new box! Oh, she was happy with herself!

I have the photo of her surrounded by those pink tissues. It made me smile then and it makes me smile now.

Littles imitate everything they see. She watched me pull that one Kleenex up, so she pulled them all up...and out. Be careful what you teach. Sometimes the things they learn from us are our bad habits. Model the behaviors that you will be happy to see them mimic.

...And, maybe set the Kleenex box where they can't reach.

Mommy, you got this!!

Mommy Moment...

Many people look back at their school year with fond nostalgia. I'm not one of them. I remember working hard to be invisible.

Kids can be ruthless when you are different. I was different. PE was the absolute worst hour of each day. I had no coordination, and no one to teach me how to play any of the sports that I loved to watch on TV with my dad. The girls in the class knew I was the "weakest link" so every day they picked and prodded. They teased and tormented. I never, by my own choice, took a shower in the locker room, although I was pushed in a few times. The thought of what new taunts would be hurled at me frightened me more than being hot and sweaty. I learned to be careful who was around me when I changed out of my gym clothes.

Oh, don't feel too bad for me. God was protecting me even in the midst. I didn't relate to kids my own age. I preferred to talk to folks my parents age or young kids. Because of that fact, I was given the opportunity to help at the grade school. I was a teacher's aide for the kindergarten classes and loved it! I also assisted the high school special education teacher, and I thrived there. To this day, teaching someone to read thrills my heart! Watching their eyes light up when the letters on a page finally come together in their mind to form words is such a joy.

I did struggle with loneliness, but God's presence became real to me, so although I don't have the fond school memories that many of you have, I look back and see the great love of God watching over me.

I pray He shows Himself to be real on your life, too.

Mommy, you got this!!

Mommy Moment...

Curt and I were going on a family vacation with our youngest three, Jenna, Kali and Caleb. We were going to Yellowstone Park for a few days. We thought that leaving directly from our day at Water World was a great plan, so that's what we did. We spent a full day in the hot sun riding water slides, and then drove to Yellowstone from there. Jen and Colton had just started dating. We had planned on him coming with her to Water World, but he had the notion that our family road trip to Yellowstone would be a great way to get to know us.

Yep. He joined us. We couldn't understand why he thought it would be fun to travel with strangers on their family vacation, but we welcomed him all the same. At least we would know right away if we liked him or not. We would know if he fit in with us.

We spent the next few days stuck in a car together. He and Jen sat in the third row together. Kali and Caleb got the middle row. Curt and I were up front. When we travel as a family we banter back and forth, we listen to odyssey CD's and we play silly car games. Colton joined right along. It didn't take but just a few days for us all six of us to start quoting movies, laughing, and throwing candy at each other across the car! He was highly entertaining. Every time we got out of the car, he would do an impression of Superman flying and dive out over the seats. When he'd get in, he'd do the same and 'fly' back over the seats.

It was an awesome time! We loved and accepted him immediately.

At some point I gave him the same advice I had given Jeff. "If you don't like the mother, don't date the daughter! You will be stuck with the mother as a part of your life forever if you marry the daughter. And, quite likely the daughter will be a just like her mother."

He still married her. His choice, I warned him. LOL

Mommy, you got this!!

Mommy Moment...

My dad was ill the last few years of his life. He was young in an era when smoking was cool, and he worked for many years in a hot, dusty, kiln firing bricks. He did quit smoking when I was quite young, but it had made his lungs weak. Doctors gave his condition some name no one could pronounce. It meant the lungs no longer allowed the oxygen into his bloodstream. At times, towards the end, he would collapse, unable to breath. It was a difficult time. If he had an "episode" while he and Mom were out, I would get a phone call telling me to go to one hospital or another. I was only twenty-five when this started to happen. It happened so often that I began to hate to hear the phone ring at all.

He was such an amazing man, and a crotchety old thing. He is the one who taught me that God was real. He was always optimistic, saying, "Could be worse." when anyone asked how he was. Right up to the end of his life. He was a stubborn old army sergeant, a World War II Vet who fought on Okinawa, and a soft-hearted teddy bear who helped me bottle feed several batches of kittens over the years. He cut and polished stones and showed me the beauty that God had hidden inside. It taught me that God put a hidden beauty in everyone… even me.

There is much to say about him, but one particular thing, I wish for you to hear.

He loved my mom, but in my lifetime, they weren't overtly loving towards each other. In today's world people walk away from marriage like they would an old car that they once treasured, but now it has a few dings and too many miles on it. People don't feel 'happy', so they divorce. That's not what Dad did. They had hard years. They had tragedy. That didn't drive them apart.

When the Doctors told us there was no hope, he lived on for several months. They could not explain how he had lived through the holidays. Nor could they explain how he lived clear through January. I can.

He made me plan an anniversary party for Mom. Her siblings and his were invited and us four kids with our families. It was a simple celebration. He sat in his chair most of the day, watching all of us, especially Mom. My sister wrote a lovely poem. It was a great day.

He died just a few days later.

That crotchety, gruff old man had lived just long enough so Mom wouldn't be grieving during the holidays and their January 30th anniversary. She would have time to grieve in February. And then, when our baby was born in March, Mom could enjoy it.

You might not believe that he could plan his time of death. I'm absolutely sure he did. He loved Mom that much. He didn't always use words to say so, but his actions did.

It's said that actions speak louder than words. I hope those around me see the things I do and know that I care. I pray that my actions show my kids that I love them.

I pray my actions show you that I care, and that you are loved.

Mommy, you got this!!

Mommy Moment...

When we had our milk cow, Honey, we referred to her as my 'therapy' cow. I could say absolutely anything to her, and she wouldn't tell a soul. I could cry and she wouldn't judge. I could vent, and she wouldn't try to fix it. She would just listen. She was my prayer partner. Many, many mornings I would pray the entire time I sat there and milked. I prayed about EVERYTHING! Friends, family, neighbors, church, and our country were all lifted up in prayer. We went through a business buyout that was quite messy, and she patiently listened to my heartfelt prayers each day. We even had a friend who was struggling for a while who would ask to come milk for me, just to have the moment of peace.

We all need that. --No. Don't run out and buy a cow. They are a lot of work.

I mean, we all need someone trustworthy and honest to listen to our hearts when the burdens get too heavy; someone who will pray with us and for us, someone to share life with us.

I believe that talking with God is vital. He has always heard my prayers, even if He hasn't answered the way I'd like. I talk to Him all day.

-My kids say I talk to myself. Maybe I do. I only do that if I want an EXPERT opinion. LOL

I've been visiting with some of you. I have heard your struggles and the hurts in your hearts. Thank you for trusting me. I am honored to listen, and happy to hear from you. I want you to know... I pray for you. I mean that. I truly do. I know that He loves you dearly!! I don't have all the answers, but I know the one who does.

Being a mommy can be overwhelming at times. I was overwhelmed quite often. I encourage you to find a time and place to visit with God.

My prayer time was never 'normal'. Few folks in this generation pray while milking a cow. Find what works for YOU. He will join you there.

And find someone you trust to talk to as well. We all need a little help sometimes.

Mommy, you got this!!

Mommy Moment...

Remodeling usually comes with its share of challenges. Ours was no exception. But we threw in an unexpected challenge.

Our church had invited a guest speaker to come preach. Curt and I volunteered to have them out for lunch. Well, that was the plan when we thought our kitchen would be finished, but it wasn't. The cupboards were in, but not the countertops. The flooring had been in, but it buckled and had to be removed and replaced...twice.

It wouldn't matter. We would just take the speaker out to dinner instead. After the service we would explain to the guest speaker and take them out to a restaurant. We had intended to let our pastor know before service about our kitchen mess and change of plans. He was busy with the logistics of the program and helping the speaker, so we didn't catch him. No worries. Right? We were just taking the guest speaker out to a restaurant. It really didn't matter if the pastor knew or not.

Turns out, it did matter. During announcements, Pastor says, " ...and the Christensen's have invited us ALL out to their house for lunch."

!!!Panic!!! I didn't hear another word. In that moment I totally forgot about the floor and countertop. My little brain started taking inventory of the food that might be in my fridge, pantry or freezer. I told Kali, who is beside me, "We will have to hustle home to get SOMETHING going for lunch. No 'doddling about' after service!" Curt said he would wait for the speaker and bring them once they finished greeting people.

Cool thing. We serve a BIG God. He didn't panic at all.

When we got home, we found a huge pan of enchiladas, a large salad and dessert. My sweet friend knew our kitchen was a mess and just thought she would bless us that day with a nice meal. She made enough for an army, because sometimes we have company. She knew nothing of the church situation.

Wow. Just Wow.

Kali and I hustled about and when our guests, all 30 or so of them, arrived, we were ready. We had a lovely meal together and a great time of fellowship. No one minded the plywood floor or plywood countertop.

We did finally get a chance to talk with our pastor…just as everyone was leaving our house.

Mommy, you got this!!

Mommy Moment…

When you live in the country sometimes you end up with random animals. Usually, it's a dog or cat that someone dumped, and it wandered into your yard. We have had it happen several times over the years.

One of our neighbors moved, but apparently, they turned loose a couple rabbits. Those rabbits found our kids' playhouse and proceeded to multiply...like rabbits...under that playhouse.

Jenna, Kali and Caleb decided to catch them. Oh, they were patient! They tried putting food out for the bunnies and waiting. But bunnies are smart...and quick. After several attempts over several days, the kids came up with a plan.

I'm not sure who thought of what, but it worked!

They tied braided twine onto the playhouse doorknob. It was a really long braid! The other end was taken up into the wooden play fort a few feet away. I can't remember if they tied it there or just held onto it. Anyway, next they put carrots inside and a trail of alfalfa leading into the playhouse. Hoping that the bunnies would come out from under the playhouse, go in for the treats and the kids could pull the string, shut the door and trap the bunnies. Bunnies are smart. They could sense the kids watching and wouldn't come out.

I told you the kids were patient. They were determined to catch those bunnies.

Soon they figured out that if they talked in normal voices the bunnies weren't afraid of them and would come out. So, the kids did just that. It took a few tries. They caught the same one several times. Then, their patience paid off and two or three went in together. They put them into an old guinea pig cage and tried again. Soon the kids had all the baby bunnies in the cage.

The kids were rewarded for their efforts. They sold those bunnies. A couple went to a friend and the others were sold to a local feed store.

Smart kids! I loved the way they worked together, and problem solved. I had no input into their plan. I didn't even help until it was time to take the sold bunnies into town. Sweet Mommy, it's good to allow your littles the opportunity to think things through by themselves. It encourages them to be responsible adults.

Mommy, you got this!!

Mommy Moment...

I had two wiggly boys. They are great men now, but as little guys they couldn't sit still. Their little minds were always processing and figuring out the world around them. They had so much enthusiasm for the world around them that their bodies were always on the move. And they were BOYS. They saw things differently than my girls. They naturally behaved differently than the girls.

I'm sure some of you have that same scenario going on in your homes. I will tell you it's ok for them to be what God created them to be, challengers, leaders, ponderers of facts, questioners of the world around them, risk takers, world changers...men.

Unfortunately, in our society today, we don't hardly know how to let boys be boys and become masculine men, gentlemen.

I am ever so grateful that God and Curt encouraged (pushed) me into homeschooling. Those busy bodies were expected to do their academics, of course, but we had the freedom to allow science to be extremely hands on. We could do math sitting outside. Our school could allow for differences in learning styles and abilities.

Both our boys are gentlemen. They are thoughtful towards those around them. Yet, when it comes right down to it, they are leaders, challengers, world changers, and risk takers.

I'd encourage you mommies to take a hard look at the expectations you have for your boy's behavior. Are their things on your list that hold them back from being men? Look at their hearts. What do they need to feel like men? My boys needed to be needed. They need some say into their schedule. They like stepping up, holding doors, carrying heavy things, being wise. I learned to treat them like men. Talk to them like men, especially as they enter the teen years.

Mommy, you got this!!

Mommy Moment...

I think he might have been three. My mom was watching Devin one day or two each week while I helped at the school. She loved that little feisty man! When I got there one day to pick him up, she shared what had happened in their day.

It seems she had given him a screwdriver. Not knowing that he knew quite well what they were for and how to use one. She thought it was adorable that he would find a screw in some table or chair and try to take the screw out. Problem was... he actually took out a few screws!

She discovered that fact when she went to sit down at the table she fell flat on the floor. He had taken out all the screws from the dinner table chairs!!

He did NOT get into any trouble. Mom thought it was hilarious!

He always had thought processing abilities that were way ahead of his physical age. As a teen we enrolled him into the local high school, but after only two years he chose not to continue. He began to take classes at the college. That same year he bought his own semi... at sixteen! He drove for Ag harvests and ran it as his own business!

If we want our boys to be good men, we have to let them BE good Godly men. We must allow them to practice that Godly manhood. Yes, they need table manners. Yes, they need to know how to do laundry for themselves. But they must be allowed to be risk takers and truth seekers. They drove toy trucks all around the house. Our boys rode their motorcycles, made forts in trees and did some things that others would call dangerous, like throwing knives at their homemade targets. I tried NOT to helicopter parent or micro-manage their days. They were LOUD, messy, active little guys.

It is difficult as a mom to decide when the behavior is acceptable and when it has gone too far. I tried to rely on God for that wisdom. I didn't always get it right. It's far too easy to expect boys to behave like girls. I am grateful that our boys got to go with Curt on a regular basis. They needed out from under mommy's care, and they needed time with Dad. They needed "guy" time.

In our world today, I think raising boys is trickier than raising girls. I pray wisdom for all of you with sweet young men in your homes.

Be wise about the tools you give them. Even little guys can figure out how to use a screwdriver.

Mommy, you got this!!

Mommy Moment...

For years Curt and I went to church in separate cars. I had to be there early, and he had to finish feeding cattle or irrigating before he could go to church. I found it annoying for a long time. It was so wasteful and ridiculous.

But our neighbors thought it was GREAT!

After church the kids could choose who they wanted to ride with. We only had Danielle and Devin at this time. I drove an old Chevy Citation. Curt drove either his 66 Mustang or his pickup.

We would race home! Truly, race. Sometimes one of us would get caught in town by a stoplight. Other times some farmer in a tractor would be going down the middle of the road and slow us down. If we came out of town together, we would pass each other and honk at each other. The kids would squeal! "Faster mommy! Don't let Daddy beat!"

We began to notice that our neighbors were outside in their yards most Sundays as we flew by. Come to find out they, too, loved the fact that we raced home, and couldn't wait to see who was winning.

We cracked a windshield doing that. But hey, we had a LOT of fun and brought a lot of joy to the kids… and to the neighborhood.

Sweet Mommy, look for ways to create a joyful atmosphere.

Mommy, you got this!

Mommy Moment...

Normally, we don't go too overboard for Valentine's Day. For many years, I made the kids some fun treat and Curt and I would go for dinner. So, when Danielle said she was coming down for Valentine's Day, I found it odd…but as you've read many times, we ARE odd.

I thought maybe we'd make cookies together or create cards. When I asked her, she said she didn't have a plan; they were just coming for lunch...odd.

Life is always more fun when the kids and grandkids are all here, so I was super excited, even if it was a bit odd for them to come for lunch in the middle of the week. Jenna, Kali and Caleb made a point to be here, too. We had a lovely time just visiting, laughing at each other and sharing stories. One thing we enjoy doing together is cooking. It's a joy filled event whenever we cook together.

Lunch was ready; Curt had come in and was washing up. The littles had set the table and were finding their places. The girls and I put the food on the table. In our house we pray before meals, so all the kids were waiting patiently ...even expectantly. Curt wasn't at the table yet. Soon, he came to the table. He knelt beside me, opened a ring case and asked me to marry him again and renew our vows. He also informed me that he was taking me on the honeymoon we never had.

I cried.

He and the kids had been planning for months! They choose the ring together. They planned the lunch together. They planned the honeymoon at a Christian couple's retreat in Hawaii together! They all worked to surprise me.

I struggle with feeling unworthy. Curt knows this. He wanted me to know that he still loved and would choose me, even after 31 years of marriage.

Your relationship with your spouse NEEDS to be a priority! Your kids are only with you temporarily. They grow up and move on. Sweet Mommy, find ways to express your love and devotion. It doesn't have to be expensive or elaborate as in this story, but it must be genuine. Tell your spouse you'd choose them again. Show them you appreciate them, do something that makes them feel special. Valentine's Day is just a good excuse to do something we should be doing every day. Tell our spouse you love them.

We've been together thirty-eight years, and I am so very blessed! I have a great man.

Mommy, you got this!!

Mommy Moment...

Pulling into the driveway I saw Devin on the 4-Wheeler. He was simply driving in a circular path around our house. Nothing unusual about WHAT he was doing. But there was something different about HOW he was doing it. Something was wrong! I hurried into the house. I was extremely worried about Devin. I had only seen him only for a moment as I drove into the yard, but something about the way he drove frightened me. I'm sorry to say, I probably came into the house as 'mama bear'.

"What's wrong with Devin?! Something is wrong! Is he sick?!"

About then we heard the 4-Wheeler roll! Devin had been driving too fast and as he rounded a corner. It flipped! He wasn't badly injured. He was just shaken up. He was more worried about the gasoline that had leaked onto him than he was of any injury.

As it turned out, he was running a fever and really was sick. Curt asked me later, how I had known something was wrong.

Truly, I couldn't answer the question. I just knew. I know my kids. His behavior was somehow different.

Kids give us all sort of clues when something isn't right. Of course, running a fever is an obvious clue, but it may be a crabby attitude. It might be dark wax in their ears. Sometimes they are just "off" and we can't quite figure out why.

I trust God to tell me when something is wrong. I'm not fearful, but I AM aware. I'm the expert on my kids. I know them better than anyone else does. Small changes in their behavior can give clues that something is wrong.

In our house if I thought a kid might be getting sick, I would pull out the humidifier, colloidal silver, the Vicks maybe even the nasal wash. If it is a respiratory issue, I add elderberry elixir. Not one of our kid's ever went to the ER... most have never been to the Dr. --We are weird. I know.

Ask God to help you have wisdom. Ask Him to teach your heart to trust Him and your motherly instincts. He loves you and He loves your kids.

Mommy, you got this!!

Mommy Moment...

You all know I couldn't cook when Curt and I got married. Well, unless you count bologna sandwiches and boxed macaroni and cheese. Add that to the fact that we were married before the internet and YouTube videos. My tools were as limited as my skills. I had one cookbook, and a few recipe cards that came as a shower gift, and sheer determination. Meals were quite...ummm...interesting some days. I so wanted to make Curt proud of me...or at least not let him starve to death.

We lived in town for the first year. He usually left early and didn't come home till supper. That gave me all day to work on a meal. -Some days it took all day.

He was so sweet! Even if it wasn't so tasty, he would eat it and praise my efforts.

But...when it came to dessert... THAT was a different story. he ate it alright, cake, cobbler, pies or puddings. He ate them all, even enjoyed them. But...as he finished them off, he'd say, "It was good...but it would be better with cream."

I had never had cream. Ice cream, sure. Not cream. Why would you need cream? Who keeps cream in the house?

Well... me. I now keep cream in the house. I have since I figured out it is a simple way to please him. I realized it really meant a lot to him. I didn't care about cream, but he did.

I am so glad that I didn't get my feelings hurt and make it a huge issue. It can be little things like this that fester in your heart that can destroy a relationship. Sure, he could have learned to eat desserts without cream on them. It's also true that I could learn to keep cream in the fridge.

Love your hubby well!! There are so many reasons to do so. If you treat him like a king, you get to be queen.

Mommy, you got this!!

Mommy Moment...

I loved being out and about with the kids! One day, there was some promotion going on at a local store. I told the kids we'd go if they got their schoolwork finished. They did. We did. Once there each of the kids won a goldfish in a bag! Live goldfish!

Oh goodie. Now we needed goldfish food and something to put them in. Next stop...somewhere that sold fish food.

We couldn't leave three bags with a fish in each one in a hot car, so we traipsed into the store **with** them. We bought fish food, but being a realist, I told the kids we'd put their fish in some bowl at home for a few days just to be sure they lived. Then we'd consider an aquarium. As we waited in the checkout line an older lady watched the kids and I interact. She was so tickled with how sweet they were to each other and how polite they were. She made quite a fuss praising them. I thanked her kindly, but said they were just normal kids.

They were about to prove me right.

We had one more stop before we could take our bagged fish home. The car needed fuel. Just before I pulled into the station the kids were fussing at each other in the back seat. I'm not real clear what took place, but Caleb's bag began to leak!

Now I have a wet kid, wet backseat and a dying fish! Yea.

Luckily, one of those polite, well behaved kids had left a small bucket in the car, so once we got to the station, I dumped the fish into the bucket. The lady was right. The kids were super polite and well behaved. Their behavior earned them praise many, many times over the years. They were given balloons, ice cream, and oh so much praise everywhere I took them, but I was right, too. They were just normal kids.

We put those goldfish into my large mixing bowl and sat them in the middle of the table. One died shortly, but one lived for YEARS! As we ate meals that little fish would swim to the side of the bowl in front of the person speaking. Eventually, a friend took pity on Finny and gave us a small aquarium.

I expected good behavior from them all, that's true. I also put a lot of time in training them to behave well. That is true, too. But my expectations weren't so high that I couldn't offer grace when things went wrong. Kids need a balance of training, expectations, and Grace.

We ALL need grace!

Mommy, you got this!!

Mommy Moment...

There's a lot of fuss about how agricultural animals are treated. I'd like to tell you a couple short stories to give you an idea of how we cared for our animals.

The snow came suddenly, and the wind with it. Within the stretch of about an hour we were in the middle of a full blizzard with well over a foot of snow. It hadn't been too bad when Curt had done chores at four. All the animals looked good and had come up to the feeders. By the time he finished chores and was working on the tractor, the weather had moved in. It was supper time by then, so he came home. After supper, the storm intensified! About 10:00 he decided to head back to check on them. It was spring and several ewes were close to delivering. I'm not kidding when I say I was afraid for him. - This was before cell phones, so there would be no contact until he made it back home.

The road between our house and the pens was just over 1/2-mile-long, but in these conditions, I didn't know how long it would take him. At 11:00 I started looking for him. By midnight I was worried. 1:00 am came and went, still no Curt. It was 2:00 before I saw him.

I cried tears of gratefulness as he sat down to take his boots off.

The snow had been drifting so badly when he left that he only made it 1/4 of the way down in the pickup. After that...he had walked! He is a brave man. He kept an eye out for the yard light and finally got down to the farmyard. Once there, he had gotten into the loader. He had to clear the road as he went, but he did make it down to the sheep barn. There he found them, snug and warm in the barn, all safe and cared for. He had put his life on the line just to be sure those ewes and lambs were safe.

That's what it's like to be a farmer.

Our kids remember most springs we'd have a few baby lambs in our kitchen. Yes. In the kitchen! Yes. They were smelly and noisy. Yes, it was inconvenient. But...It was the best place for them while we nursed them back to health. I'd be up every two hours for weeks with different babies, checking their temperatures, feeding them and for some of them holding them on my shoulder and patting them until the fluid in their lungs cleared and they could breathe again.

I know parents who complain if they have to be up in the night with their own kids. How about spending a month or two getting little to no sleep in the care of little lambs that have little chance of survival? That's what farm families do!

Our animals are cared for, prayed for, and often times put first before our own families, and our own needs, and our own safety. We never mistreat an animal. We want them happy and healthy. We love them well!

Our kids learned compassion for animals, how to put others first, how to work hard, and the importance of every life.

Mommy, you got this!!

Mommy Moment...

We were expecting our second child. I was worried about how our 2-year-old would respond to having a new baby. Frankly, I was worried about how I would respond. Don't get me wrong. I was so excited! It's just that I'd never had two kids before.

Anyhow, I tried to think of ways to help Danielle adjust to having to share my attention with a sibling. God reminded me of a book I'd had as a child "Baby Dear". In it the family gives a doll to the older child when a new baby joins the family.

That's what we did. I had a doll made for Danielle. The day I delivered Devin; we gave her the doll. We also gave her baby bottles, diapers and clothes for her 'baby". When I nursed my baby, she fed hers. When I changed my baby, she changed hers.

I really don't know if it helped her adjust, but I do know we never had any issues. After a few weeks, she was far more interested in helping me than she was in mimicking me. She was marvelous help! Because of the way we handled the situation, she adored Devin. Unintentionally we taught her HOW to take care of a real baby. She knew how to hold him, how to feed him, she could even change a wet diaper proficiently. It was awesome. That little 2 1/2-year-old was amazing!

I learned just how easy it can be to train a child to be helpful. I didn't demand. I didn't give direct instruction. I shared my day. I showed her how and allowed her to learn at her own pace. Once she knew what to do and how, I let her help with her baby brother.

Yes, I did let her feed and care for Devin as much as she was capable.

The experience became the pattern of our parenting, show, teach, help, and allow them to do it. Our kids were, and are, very capable, and it all started with a little book my mother read to me...and God reminding me of it.

Mommy, you got this!!

Mommy Moment...

Every spring our youth leader planned a ski trip with the kids. It was quite an undertaking. We would work with the youth group kids all year, helping them earn enough money to go skiing. They were super excited. We all were. I think there were 25 or so kids and 10 or 12 adults.

That morning as Curt and I were loading up our own little family Devin came to me and asked about a zit he had.

He was only 10 or 11 years old. He didn't have zits. Yep. Chicken Pox! I wanted to cry.

Curt and I talked it over. I was the cook for the whole group. Staying home wasn't really an option for me. We decided that Curt would stay home with him and the rest of us (1 teen, 2 littles and I) would go on the trip.

I hate leaving a sick kid. I had never had to do that before. I cried. I didn't sleep. I nearly made myself sick worrying about him. -This was pre cell phones, so I couldn't check in on him.

Funny thing. He was fine. He was happy as a lark and hardly bothered by the pox. Add that to the fact that since Daddy was the one spending time with him, he got to watch movies all day and go out to McDonald's every day, he was MARVELOUS! He did miss skiing, but he had quite enjoyed his time with Dad.

Sometimes I forget that I'm not the only parent. I don't remember that I don't have to be responsible for everyone all the time. I married a great man. He may not do things the same way as I would do, but he always takes good care of us. I certainly would NOT have done fast food every day, but what a fun memory to share with Dad.

It's ok, Sweet Mommy, to let Daddy be Daddy. The kids will be just fine…so will you.

Mommy, you got this!!

Mommy Moments…

Kids go through various stages as they grow, some physical, some emotional. It's all part of maturing. I don't mean long term bad behavior. I'm referring to a short moment in time when they are attempting to become independent people and they do something out of character.

When our older son was in the "I don't want to be hugged by my mom" stage, our youngest was in the "my parents are the best, I ALWAYS want a hug" stage. There are twelve years and two sisters between those two.

When saying goodnight one-night Devin said he didn't want a hug. Although it made me a bit sad, I understood and didn't push. He was a boy, becoming a man. I had to treat him like a man. He wasn't disrespectful. Just learning to assert himself a bit.

Problem was that Caleb heard it. It truly hurt his heart. He came and jumped into my arms, "It's ok, Mommy. I ALWAYS hug yous!!!"

Even now to write this I can hear the sincerity in his little sweet voice. The memory is sweet. It makes me cry.

Devin got through that stage; don't you worry. Once he went to college, he was a hugger again and when we were out in public he LOVED to walk with my arm through his. That's memory is sweet as well.

My point is…they go through stages. Let them. Don't take offense. It may be something they say in public, or something they do. Hold fast to the truth: you love them, they love you. Their hearts come back around. I promise.

Mommy, you got this!!

Mommy Moment…

My mom used "Dolly" as a term of endearment for everyone she cared about. I can still hear her voice in my head. I, like my mom, use "Dolly" when speaking to my girls and my granddaughters. Honestly, I probably use it for any young lady I care about. "Bud" for my guys. "My little love" "Honey" and "Sweetie" are all common terms in my vocabulary.

We all have phrases and words that we repeat often. I had a few sayings that I said to my kids. I thought I'd share them with you guys.

"Tut, tut. It looks like rain." When someone was upset and might try to use tears to manipulate. According to my kids I said this nearly daily.

"Naughty things happen when you do naughty things." It's another way of saying "think about the consequences". I also said it after the fact, when they were trying to get sympathy for a bad choice. This is the one I think I said daily. Caleb says it's the one that kept him from doing naughty things. It played over in his head when he considered misbehaving.

"Is your problem with me?" I used this one anytime our kids tried to complain about another one's behavior.

The one I said most often in the car was, "We are NOT the Bickerson's." It was at times accompanied by a tap on the breaks. I often followed it with, "Speak nicely"- Kali now tells me her thought when I'd say this was, "No duh." But she never said that as a child.

"Is that duplicatable?" This came in handy whenever I thought what they were doing was a bit dangerous. It also applied when an older kid wanted something that wasn't a great idea for a little brother or sister.

Why I am writing this, you might ask. Well, your words will play over in their heads. Good or bad. Pleasant words or words filled with anger. Your words will stick with them. God says the tongue is like the rudder of a ship. I think our words steer our kid's lives. It's easy to speak without thinking. I'd encourage you to think about the words you use. Many kids struggle with negative words playing over in their heads. As parents we need to find positive words to pour into our kid's hearts and minds as often as we can. It's not easy, but it is simple. It means taking a breath when you want to speak. Sometimes it means walking away when the wrong words are on the tip of your tongue. The power of life and death are in our words. Speak life, Sweet Mommy.

Mommy, you got this!!

Mommy Moment...

I don't often share this. Please read with mercy.

The day I realized I was pregnant with our 5th; I was a mess. It had been less than a year since Curt's father had died suddenly. Six months previous I had discovered my mom (in her 70's) was being abused by the man that she had recently married. And then, mom had been killed in a car accident about four months before that day. We'd had so much tragedy. Then there is the fact that the daughter of the man who married my mom was challenging the estate and trying to get money that had been my dad's. Needless to say, I was a mess.

I'm ashamed to say I didn't want to be pregnant. I argued with God for a couple of months. We had four kids. The stress of losing Mom, selling her house, hiring a lawyer, tending our home, consoling our kid's as they grieved...it made me such an emotional mess. I struggled… so I kept arguing with God. I said some terrible things to Him.

While I was at church working on some youth group plans a friend came in. She happened upon me in the hallway. I say friend, but what happened next put that to the test.

This lady proceeded to tell me I had no right to have five kids. I already had four! I shouldn't have gotten pregnant! If I knew what caused pregnancy, I'd have stopped it! Words, oh such hate filled words! More words kept coming at me! Louder! More accusing. I was shocked. I couldn't think. I had to get away! I turned toward the steps and ran out the door. She followed. Still more words. All at once I had words of my own!

"We can have as many kids as God gives us. Yes. I DO know how pregnancy happens!" I answered her accusations and hurried to my car. I quickly drove away, fuming the whole time. How dare she say such things!

Then God spoke. He asked me what the difference was between what she said to me compared to what I, myself, had been saying to Him. Ouch!

It was true. Her words were nearly identical to my own.

I'm actually grateful for her. I never understood why she did it, but it caused me to repent of the horrible things I had said to God about the sweet babe I was carrying. From that day forward I prayed for that baby. I begged God to bless him and not hold my bad attitude against him. Thankfully, God is a good God. He definitely blessed that sweet babe.

It was a terrible moment in time. It cost her my friendship. I think she felt guilty for what she said and couldn't face me after that. But God turned it into good. He softened my heart and turned my emotions around.

I am truly grateful for her.

Once I got over my bad attitude, I was all "mama bear" about the sweet baby I was carrying. I told you that I realized I was pregnant just a few months after my mom's accident. What I didn't say was that I was due exactly one year after her death, almost to the day. And, although one friend was no help, another one held me tight. She encouraged me. She teased me. She watched over my heart.

God has a funny way of looking out for me. He knew I would struggle when we got to the 1-year anniversary of Mom's death. So, it just happened that our church was holding Vacation Bible School that particular week. I LOVE VBS! I'm all in when it comes to kids' hearts. It truly helped me emotionally to have something to focus on.

I was due in June. Traditionally, VBS is held the first week of school break in June. That meant I was due that same week. My sweet friend kept a close eye on me... as did all the teens in our youth group. They LOVED watching my stomach "roll-over."

Never has there been a mom with more 'mother hens' watching over her.

I have super quick deliveries (don't hate me) so when my friend wanted to plan a trip to the Denver Zoo that same week to celebrate her son's birthday, I questioned my sanity; a week of VBS, then a trip to the Zoo, all while I'm 9 months pregnant?!?!

I said sure. I love the zoo and any trip with her, is a blast!

No. I did NOT deliver at the church. No. Not at the Zoo either, but I was having some contractions strong enough to stop me in my tracks while there. She threatened to take me to the Zoo's nursery SEVERAL times.

Our baby waited till all the busyness was over, and then Friday night at about 10:30 he arrived.

I can tell you that although my attitude wasn't the best at first, God blessed us with the perfect gift at the perfect time! I may question God at times, but I do trust that He wants my best...even when I can't understand what He is doing. He wants the very best for you, too!

Mommy, you got this!!

Mommy Moment...

Devin chose to go to The Honor Academy near Tyler, Texas for ministry training. That is a LONG drive from our home! Our three youngest were always good travelers, but eleven or so hours in a car can be hard on the best of folks, and especially on little folks.

I planned to take books on CD, car games, puzzle books and even the lap looms that we made, but nothing I packed brought joy to the kids like the things my niece sent along. That dear girl sent eleven wrapped gifts: one gift for each hour in the car.

She wrapped all sorts of things, snacks, toys, puzzles. Each hour one of the kids was allowed to open one package. We took turns as to who opened them. We started from the youngest and worked up.

They were delighted! It didn't matter if there were three juice boxes or three toy rings, the anticipation and guessing what might be in the next gift occupied them the whole way there.

If the kids had thought there would-be black licorice or cooked liver in those gifts, they would NOT have been excited to open them, but they knew the gift giver and knew she loved them.

Life can be like that. If we trust that God will have sweet things planned for us, we can have joy and excitement for each new day. He is the ultimate gift giver and loves us dearly. We can trust Him to have good gifts in store for us. Even if the road is long and the journey is hard, He will have good gifts for us along the way.

What good gifts did you 'open' today?

Mommy, you got this!!

Mommy Moment...

There was no money left in the savings, not any. I had been to town and paid a couple bills, the checking account was down to the minimum balance. We had been trusting God and trying to do the right thing. Now...we had no money. I'm pretty frugal, but we were done.

I was driving home that day. It was July 2nd. I was crying and shouting at God while I drove...

I'd say I was praying, but that isn't quite honest. If you'd have heard me, I'm sure you would NOT have thought it sounded like prayer.

...I told Him all the facts and let Him know He had to fix it quick or we wouldn't be able to pay bills that month. He had to do something!

By the time I got home I felt a little better. I got my act together and went into the house with my few groceries. I didn't want the kids to see that I'd been crying. We hadn't told anyone just how bad it was, not even them.

On the 3rd a neighbor stopped by. He explained that he needed a bit of help getting some farm work done. He asked if Curt would be free to help him out a bit. He'd be happy to pay Curt for his time...

I cried! I waited till he left, went into our bathroom. Sat on the floor and cried.

No one knew what an answer to prayer that was except Curt and me.

I would have preferred that God answer our earlier prayers, but He answered in His perfect timing.

It's easy to SAY we trust Him, but do we? Really? If I really trusted Him, I probably wouldn't have been praying so loudly that day in the car.

I don't know. Maybe it's ok to say loud prayers, to be honest about your needs and pain. I sure hope so. I figure He already knows the situation and how I feel about it, so being honest about it doesn't shock Him. And, the Bible does say that we should pray about everything and in all situations, so... I think its ok.

I will forever be grateful for our neighbor, and the answered prayer!

Mommy, you got this!!

Mommy Moment...

When the kids were little, I was not their friend. I was Mommy, sometimes Mother, and occasionally Mama Bear, but not Friend. They knew that I adored them and would do anything for them, but they also knew that I wanted them to be Godly men and women when they were adults.

The years of training and parenting have passed so quickly. Today, we are friends. We respect each other and enjoy being together.

When we are out together it's funny to watch other people watch us interact.

Let me give a couple of examples...

Caleb and I were out grocery shopping. We had been teasing and laughing all throughout the store. While loading our items into the car, a lady approached us. Unbeknownst to us, she had been watching and listening to us as she had been loading her child into her car next to us. "I hope I have that kind of relationship with MY son when he grows up." Her words were so kind, so heartfelt, and so sweet.

The girls and I enjoy shopping...no surprise there. We enjoy the few times when it works out for all of us to shop together. Flicking through the racks, teasingly recommending clothes for one another, we will hear some snickering and look up to see the ladies nearby watching us. More than once, they've commented on what a fun family we are or how sweet it is to hear us interact.

While taking family photos several years back Devin scooped me up. The photographer snapped the shot of him holding me in his arms. Caleb did just the same thing THIS year. Both times the photographer laughed at us.

Today, while shopping with Kali, the lady at the fitting rooms who said she loved seeing us at the store! We don't go there often. I don't believe I've ever seen her before, but she told another clerk that she always enjoys it when we come in.

Parenting littles seem monotonous and tiring. I know, Sweet Mommy. Those years pass all too soon. The rewards of intentional parenting are tremendous! You may feel like the mean mom at times. You may even have to *be* her occasionally but keep your heart set on the goal: the goal of having amazing, Godly adults who call you mom. There is no greater reward.

Mommy, you got this!!

Mommy Moment...

Bouncing off the walls! Ever feel like your kids are bouncing off the walls? I did. Since we homeschooled and were together 24/7, I was totally aware of changes in their behaviors. Sure, there were days when I felt they were off the hook!

I'm slow. I'm sorry to say, it took me a long time to connect all the dots.

I cooked every day, three meals every day! Sometimes I was tired. We couldn't afford to eat out, or order in pizza. Sometimes it was easier to eat cereal for breakfast or open a box of corn dogs for lunch. I soon noticed that the days I served cereal, those were the days that the kids, especially the boys, were off the hook. They couldn't focus. They couldn't sit still. They just couldn't seem to behave.

It took a while, but once I saw the connection, I began to test it. I'd serve cereal and observe how our day went.

Yep. You got it. It always corresponded with bad days.

I began to change our eating habits. In today's terms...we went keto... well mostly. We had protein at every breakfast. We had quality foods at all our meals. We still love chips and ice cream, but we limit them to once a week or less.

I tell you this to help some of you sweet mothers who can't figure out why you and your kids have bad days. It CAN be as simple as the foods you all eat. There are many things that play into bad behavior...lack of sleep, poor training, hurt heart, or sometimes sugar overload.

I'd love to see you try to serve meat, and real high fat non-sugary yogurt or eggs for breakfast. --Eggs are cheap and can be made all kinds of wonderful ways. I don't want to add to the challenge of parenting. I truly want to help you all. My own boys had great hearts and wanted to be good. I feel awful that I was clueless.

I hope it helps even one of you. Nutrition really does matter.

Mommy, you got this!!

Mommy Moments...

Easter morning is a joyous time! Our family has always gone to church on Easter. We feel is important to start that Sunday (and most other Sundays) celebrating Christ.

It was little busy when we volunteered with the youth group. Our teens, Curt and I all had to be at church early enough to make and serve Easter Breakfast for the whole church. That meant being there around 5:30 am…two teens and three littles and ourselves dressed, hair done, and ready before church. Doable, just challenging. Now throw in helping with the sunrise service. - Still not horrible, just 30 minutes earlier.

Add the time change. That's like 4am! You're talking getting up at 3am! - Stop there. That's not normal!

True, but it is what we did. The time change corresponded with Easter more than once during those years. One was memorable…

Our girls have super thick, fast growing, and beautiful hair. The two younger girls were just little when they heard about Locks of Love, a ministry that made and donated wigs to young cancer patients. Every other year just before Easter we would cut and donate their hair. That particular year I had promised to cut it before Easter, but we had been extra busy in the weeks before Easter and hadn't gotten around to cutting their hair.

Kali came into the church kitchen that early Easter morning with such a sad look on her face. "Mommy, we didn't cut my hair." She looked and sounded so pitiful. She was heartbroken that I had broken my promise.

I knew I could rationalize and explain to her why we hadn't done it, but I also knew it genuinely broke her heart to have forgotten. In her eyes, we had forgotten those kids who needed the wigs, and I had broken my promise to cut it before Easter. I found some scissors, took her out of the kitchen, braided her hair...and cut it, just like I had promised.

What would you have done? Gotten frustrated and snapped at her? Patted her on the head and shuffled her out the door? Ignored her?

You're right. I could have done any of those. It wouldn't really matter. We couldn't mail it until Monday. But, you see, I had made a promise. I had given my word. Sure, I could've made an excuse, but the price of making that excuse would be my sweet, kind-hearted girl's broken heart.

It wasn't worth that price. It's easy to make promises to kids. It's easy to excuse breaking such promises. To me, the price was always too great.

I was careful what I promised our kid's. Trust is easily broken, and far more difficult to repair.

Mommy, you got this!!

Mommy Moment...

My mom worked outside of the home from the time I was tiny. At first, Dad worked nights and stayed with me during the days. Mom worked days and spent evenings with me. After leaving Denver, she worked late into the evening. We never saw much of one another because I left early for school. I'm sure she felt I was slipping away. She had a good friend advise her to find some way to connect with me.

In today's world she might have taken me for coffee, or maybe a manicure. 40+ years ago those weren't common things to do.

Instead, Mom started playing cards with me each morning before school, for maybe 15 or 20 minutes depending on when she got up. Canasta was the game we played. Quite often I had to leave for school in the middle of a hand. We'd set the cards in the middle of our old round table, pick them up the next morning, and continue our game.

Some might think it an odd thing, but my mom was truly wise. Yes, we played cards, but it gave us a chance to connect, to have fun together. We talked about whatever came to mind. We connected in a positive way. It was the beginning of the loving bond we had in the years that followed.

When you are a mommy to teens it can be hard to connect. As mommies we can struggle with teens who are trying to grow up. It might be good to step back and find something that you can do together: maybe a craft, or gardening, maybe it will be going to coffee. It might be playing card games.

Their hearts need you, even if their actions or words seem to push you away. I NEEDED my mom to care. I had become self-sufficient out of necessity, but my heart was hurting. She never attended parent teacher conferences, or any play I was in, but she DID find a way to make me feel important to her.

Sweet Mommy, your kids need a heart connection with you...no matter how young or old they might be.

Mommy, you got this!!

Mommy Moment...

Well, my life hasn't been a fairy tale.

That's what I told a dear friend today. It's played over and over in my head since I said it. It sounds like a complaint. It was really just a statement. I hadn't meant to complain.

Not a fairy tale? Hmmm...

In a fairy tale you usually have an underdog, someone who struggles to see good in themselves. They usually have a tough go of it at first. Sometimes, they are teased or bullied. Then you have a hero who changes the way the underdog sees himself. There is always a crisis, sometimes a series of tragedies. In the end the guy gets the girl, and all is well.

I guess I do live in a fairy tale.

I was a mess as a kid, teased, bullied, and headed the wrong way. Curt came into my life when no one thought I'd amount to much. He helped me see the best in me. He took me to church where I could meet Jesus. He taught me how to be a capable mother, farm hand and wife. Sure, our lives had conflict and challenges. We even had a series of tragedies.

In the end we still have each other, Jesus, five great kids, eight grandkids (so far). We have friends, dear friends, all over the world. We've had the opportunity to meet several famous people and traveled to amazing countries. We've seen tremendous miracles. We've loved and served those whom God put around us.

What else is needed to be a fairytale? Mice sewing me a dress?

I've been so very blessed! I don't need a crown on my head or a castle to live in. I'm perfectly happy with my hair in a ponytail and my farmhouse to invite people into.

If life had been easier, I wouldn't be where I am. I wouldn't understand the people around me who hurt. If money hadn't been so tight, I wouldn't have the amazing kids I have. I would have spoiled them. If I hadn't had challenges, I wouldn't have clung to God with all my might.

I guess, I *do* live in a fairytale. I'm the queen here and I'm perfectly content with that.

We all are the queens of our castles. Straighten your tiara, live with grace and mercy, and enjoy the life you've been given.

Mommy, you got this!!

Mommy Moment...

Kali and I enjoy each other's company. Shopping together is always fun, but sometimes we are quite clueless of what's going on around us.

We jumped in my car and headed out. That particular day, we were just out for groceries and a few other things. We had a joyful time teasing one another as we filled the cart. Checkout was as uneventful as usual. That's when the trouble started...

We pushed our cart straight to the car. It was a lovely sunny day. I had forgotten that I locked it, so Kali went to the driver's door and punched in the code. -We have one of those keypads on the door, so I don't get myself locked out, and have to call Curt to rescue me. But it didn't work. She started the code over...click. She had started over and halfway thru it unlocked? ...weird.

It was more than just weird.

I reached for the hatch door, just as she returned to the back of the car to help me.

According to her, I had my hands in the air and was backing away from the car.

It's not ours! We just broke into someone's car!!!

I slammed the hatch. She locked the doors, and we stepped away... quickly! Laughing and looking suspicious.

We were puzzled. How could we have mistaken the car for ours? How did the code work? Did anyone see us?!

There was a large black pick-up next to that car. Our car was on the other side of the pickup. We were SOO close.

We put our things in, hopped in and swiftly drove away.

We have laughed and laughed at our adventure that day. So, if you didn't break into your neighbor's car today...it was a great day.

Mommy, you got this!!

Mommy Moment...

We were new to the church. We'd been going for a few weeks. We had made a few friends but hadn't met the pastor yet. Oh, we shook his hand after church, but we didn't really know him.

They had some special dinner in their fellowship hall that day. We sat down as a family at a round table. The table was full, all but two seats. The pastors noticed us and asked to join us. Introductions naturally followed, then small talk. When he asked about our plans after church, one of the kids replied that it was my birthday, and we had plans to celebrate that.

He was genuinely interested. "One of those BIG birthdays?" he asked. "One with a zero in the middle?"

"Yes." I answered...with a straight face and slight snicker.

"Wow. You look GOOD for your age!" His wife said with a grin.

About then he realized his mistake. The poor man was horrified!!

That was the beginning of a sweet friendship.

Sometimes our mistakes are blessings. Others need to see our imperfections, so that they can be honest with their own. I pray that my mistakes and mishaps bring you joy, and help you laugh at your own.

Mommy, you got this!!

Mommy Moment...

Sometimes don't you feel like making the kids go outside and then locking the doors!? Well...I did. Not only that, but I did it.

When they'd been cooped up in the house for a few days, maybe during a blizzard, or we'd been doing school testing. They'd get loud and rowdy in the house. Which is fine for a while, but let's be real, it does become too much some days.

I sent them out. They came up with an excuse to come back in. Again, I would send them out. Again, they would be back in.

So, I shuffled them back out and I locked the door.

Keep in mind, we live in the country and they had lots of things to do outside, we have three outside doors, and... I'm sure the statute of limitations is up by now. LOL

It was lovely outside... beautiful spring day. We had had a bit of rain just the day before. I kept an eye on them through my large picture window.

Finally, I had a moment of quiet! Only a moment though. Pretty soon, I hear squealing. I hurry to the door. There my three sweet littles are playing in the huge puddle that the rain created. I should say playing in the mud hole! Our driveway is maybe, 40 feet long and 20 feet wide, and the water was maybe 6 or 8 inches deep.

When they start something, they are ALL IN! Yep. Head to toe! And there in the middle stood the squealer. She "lost a shoe" and is STUCK standing there in the middle of the mud hole.

Me: Just walk out.

Her: I can't! I lost my shoe!

Me: You are already muddy.

Her: But I lost my shoe! I'm stuck!

No more quiet moment.

I waded out. I scooped her up. Put her on dry ground and went and found the shoe. It really was stuck, sucked right down in the mud.

I think we all act that way at times. I know I do. I get something in my head and can't see the oh, so simple answer. Thankfully, God has always rescued me.

Mommy, you got this!!

Mommy Moment...

My in-laws were out of town. Myself and my two littles were checking on their house, just making sure everything was ok while they were gone. I was doing a walk through. Dani and Devin were following along. I didn't know that the cat had followed us in.

I had checked the bedroom windows and was heading down the hallway to the living room.

I didn't see it happen, but I sure heard it…a horrible, frightening THUD!

My heart stopped.

I turned to see my sweet son laying on the floor dazed. He had tripped over the cat and slammed his forehead into the sharp edge of the door jam.

We've all seen the cartoons where someone gets hit on the head and a large lump suddenly grows up from the spot. That's what it was like.

I ran to him, scooped him up and hurried to the kitchen to get ice. In that time a "goose egg" appeared on his head! I so wanted to scream, or at very least cry, but I had to stay calm. I didn't want to frighten him, or Danielle. I was so scared! It kept growing! I thought the skin would burst!

I calmly as I possibly could. I gathered the kids, locked the door, and quickly drove the 3\4 miles to the shop where Curt was. I needed him to look at it. I needed his calm presence. I so needed him to look me in the eye and tell me Devin would be ok, that I hadn't killed my child.

That sounds silly when I write it. But truly I mean it. I needed Curt's reassurance. I was a young mommy, maybe 22 at this point. I had never seen such a wound.

Curt was calm, and oh so kind. He reassured my heart. By now the "goose egg" had stopped growing and looked less frightening.

Devin was fine. He didn't even have a headache once we got home. I made him rest for a bit, but shortly he was off playing.

God wants us to run to Him, the way I ran to Curt. I knew I could trust Curt. I knew He wanted to help me. God's like that, too. I could've beaten myself up for being a horrible mom. Curt reminded me that I was a good mommy, and he loved me, even when bad things happened. God feels that way about you, too, Sweet Mommy.

Mommy, you got this!!

Mommy Moment...

I've learned through many life lessons that God knows what I need before I need it. In this case our old car got to the point where I had to slam the door just as I turned the key to start it. You can't imagine the funny looks I got when we were out in public and I'd do it two or three times because I didn't time it right. We needed a new car.

I had only one feature I required in the new car. It had to have the "New" feature of shoulder belts for the back seats. Curt chose the car we could afford with that one feature. We purchased a "new to us" car. I was thrilled NOT to have to slam the door to start the car.

Devin was with my mom that day. I was picking Danielle up from school...

Yes, we homeschooled our kid's, but not until Danielle was to start 3rd grade.

...Danielle got into the back-passenger seat, and we were off! It was always a treat to get one-on-one time with her. I glanced at the rear-view mirror as I stopped to make my turn, just in time to realize the kid behind us wasn't paying attention. We were going to get hit!

It's weird. My brain went into some fast calculations. I knew I'd have to swing wide as oncoming traffic passed, so as not to hit someone else. I also knew to remove my foot from the brake, so we'd be a rolling target. At that point I paused and waited for impact. My mind listened for Danielle's shoulder belt to 'click' signifying it had locked as we were hit.

Our brains are so amazing!

We did get hit, but neither of us were injured in anyway. I was so very thankful for that shoulder belt in the back seat. God knew ahead of time, what car we would need.

It took me a while to be comfortable driving again. The insurance provided a loaner car for the weeks it took to get our fixed.

Actually, God gave us an extra blessing because of the accident. The back end of the car was more than a tiny bit mangled. When the body shop took out the back seat, they found a lovely opal ring underneath it. The car had previously been owned by a rental company, and they had no way to track down the ring's owner, so I was allowed to keep it. I still have that ring.

God held us close that day, and He continues to do so.

Mommy, you got this!!

Mommy Moment...

Faint voice on the phone: I'm ok. I'm ok. Mommy come get me. I'm ok...

What a frightening moment it is when you hear your child's voice calling out and you know something is HORRIBLY wrong. It was Jenna on the line, and she was definitely NOT ok.

Me: Jenna. Where are you?

Jenna: I'm ok. I'm in the slough. I'm ok. I'm ok...

Her voice faded off. I ran to the door. Grabbed a pair of shoes. Shouted back into the house, "Stay here! Kali, call Dad. Tell him to meet me in the slough. Call Dani and Devin. Tell them to PRAY!!!!!!!!!!!" The poor girl had no idea what had just happened or where I was going, but she did as I asked.

I started for my car. Jenna had blocked it in with hers. I tried hers. No keys! She had taken her keys with her. The only other vehicle in the yard was the old Jeep Cherokee that the kids used around the farm. It didn't always go into gear, the brakes barely worked, and it steered all funky. But… It was 4 wheel-drive, and the key was in it.

Off I went. Shouting at God the whole time. Yes. Others might say praying, but it was loud and fervent!

I paused when I reached our irrigation pivot. I realized I really didn't know where Jen was for sure. The farm has a couple of slough areas, one to my left and one directly in front of me, but each a half mile from that pivot. I shouted at God. I never expected an answer…especially not an audible one.

That's when a small voice from the back seat directed me to the one in front of us. I nearly jumped out of my skin! In my panic I hadn't realized that Caleb had gotten in with me. He was in the back seat. "Oh, God help me," I prayed. Now my momma heart was torn between protecting this little 10-year-old from whatever scene we were about to find, and at the same time, I was so very grateful for his help. I needed his eyes to help me find her. He was right about the slough. She would have called the other one The Pond.

The shortest distance between me and the place where I thought Jenna was meant driving through a field, which normally would not be an issue, but it was being plowed at that very moment. That means the soil was freshly turned to a depth of a foot, and extremely soft! I kept going. I sped through the farmyard with all the speed this momma bear could get out of that old jeep.

As I passed the shop, I saw Curt heading for his pickup. Kali had called him.

I had just turned toward the main slough. It covered at least 5 or 6 acres (more than a city block) She could be anywhere. Again, with the shouted prayers, "God, I don't even know where she is! Help me!"

"Is that a log? Right there?"

My mind puzzled. What was that? Was it Jenna?! "Oh, God, no," my heart prayed. What looked like a log in the water was actually Jenna.

The next second made my heart stop and took my breath away. There lay Jenna…face down in the water. "Oh, God. No. Please help me!!" I prayed.

"Stay here, Caleb!" ---He didn't.

Jenna truly was face down in the water. Apparently, she had been driving around the slough to see a new bunch of hatchlings when something caught in her front tire and threw her. The motorcycle flew up and crashed about 20 feet according to her tracks. She flew that far, also.

She had scrapes, bruises and swelling from head to toe on her left side. She is a tough girl though. In her pain and confusion, she had still managed to stand the cycle up, attempt to start it, recalculate, call me, take her shoes and socks off and lay in the water to cool her injuries.

Here are the miraculous parts of this story: 1) I was home to get the call 2) I had to drive the only one of the vehicles that could have made it through that plowed field. 3) Caleb was there to assist 4) We went to the right place 5) She was coherent enough to make a call and cool those wounds.

Then there is the phone itself. A couple days after the accident, I took her phone in to get a new one and transfer her data over to it. The tech there swore it was impossible that her phone made a call after the crash. It was completely smashed and would never have made a call. The second tech agreed, as did their manager. But it DID make that call.

We have seen so many miracles in our lives, but this one (or series of them) is the one that still will drop me to my knees. God saved this girl at birth and continues to watch over her carefully.

I pray that you never receive a call like this one, but if you do...May God work miracles for you.

Mommy, you got this!!

Mommy Moment...

We ate together 3 meals a day most of the time. We didn't really have assigned seats at the table, but we are creatures of habit and it did work out that we usually sat in the same places. Sitting at the table together at mealtimes was an absolute blessing...most of the time.

Devin sat across the table from me. One morning he and his friend were enjoying a late breakfast after a sleepover. I'd made them pancakes.

I looked up from my own breakfast to see Devin shoving a HUGE bite into his cute little face! I was a bit horrified. He had good manners. Really! He did. I started to get after him. When I glanced over to his friend, what did I see?

The kid was shoving literally half the pancake into his mouth!!

Kids are kids. I didn't get after either of them. I didn't see the point. They weren't being naughty. They were just being kids.

There is a time and place to teach and hold to rules. There are other times when we mommies need to smile, shake our heads and laugh. Learning the difference is what makes a good mommy great.

My own learning curve was great. I made lots of mistakes. I pray that God uses my mistakes to help and encourage you.

Mommy, you got this!!

Mommy Moment...

We don't buy packaged foods. As the kids were growing up, we just couldn't afford them. Because of that, I learned to love cooking, especially with the kids as my helpers.

I say I "learned" to love, because it wasn't a natural gift, to say the least. I have made cookies that had too much salt, I've made super flat ones, I've burned more batches than most of you've probably made. Cakes have overflowed their pans, burned in the bottom of the oven and filled the house with smoke. I've over-cooked steaks. I've under-cooked potatoes. And bread? I have ruined so many loaves of bread! Yeast was NOT my friend! It took me so very long to work with yeast. Some loaves didn't raise, others overflowed all over the counters.

Why do you care? Well, you may be stuck at home cooking and baking with your kids. If you are comfortable in a kitchen, no problem; if cooking isn't your thing, no worries; I'd encourage you to give it a try.

Find a recipe site, or a YouTube video. Gather your kids and let them help you. Littles can hand you the ingredients. Older kids can read the recipe or watch the video with you. Laugh. Make a mess. Enjoy some time together.

I didn't stop cooking or baking or let the many failures discourage me. I so wanted to take good care of my family that I kept trying. Now, when people compliment something I've made, I secretly laugh. They have NO idea how far I've come!

--Just so you know, my girls had a special vinyl sign created for me a few years back. It read, "Countless people have eaten in this kitchen and gone on to lead *mostly* normal lives."

Kids! Sometimes they are a bit too honest.

Mommy, you totally got this!!

Mommy Moment...

My family has been so supportive and helpful in the writing of these stories. They have edited my grammar, corrected the facts, and even suggested stories. I am grateful.

Well, I WAS grateful until the other day.

Curt was at work. He sent me a text saying he and the guys were headed to town to go to lunch together. That's pretty normal for them on Fridays.

Ten minutes later I received another text. It read…

Car wreck

Nothing more. My heart started to race, and my overactive imagination took off!

I responded, "You?"

Another 10 minutes passed. I'm praying like mad for my hubby and the guys who work with him. Then, his response finally comes.

"No. Years ago. For your stories. Sorry, didn't mean to scare you."

I simultaneously was relieved and wanted to strangle him.

No. I didn't strangle him. It really just made me laugh. Oh, how I do love that guy!

Men think differently than women. Sweet Mommy, there will be moments when you are just so aggravated. Pause, take a deep breath and remember how much you love him. Remind yourself how lost you'd be without him. Then, shake your head, smile and say a prayer of thankfulness.

Mommy, you got this!!

Mommy Moment...

We all like new clothes, right? I'm rather tall. Hand-me-downs don't usually work for me, but Curt has a cousin who happens to be about my height. She blessed me with a huge box full of clothes! I hadn't purchased any new clothes for quite a while! When the box came, I was beside myself with joy. I took each article of clothing out one by one.

You'd have thought I was a three-year-old with a bunch of Christmas presents. I got so wrapped up in having something new that I completely ignored Danielle and Devin for a bit.

I thought I should rinse the clothes in the washer because she said they had been packed away for a while, so I sorted the clothes and threw the first load into the washer.

The morning passed quickly. Danielle needed to eat lunch and get ready for school. She was in afternoon kindergarten. I switched the laundry and sat the kids down for lunch. When we finished, I thought I'd grab the clothes out of the dryer before I brushed Dani's hair for school.

My heart sank as I opened the dryer and found that a handful of crayons must have been in the dryer. Every piece of clothing I took out had melted crayon on it. I cried. I knew it was my own fault. I must not have noticed them in the dryer when I put the clothes in, but why? Why hadn't I seen them? Why had the kids put them in there? Why couldn't I have something nice and new? I cried more.

I realized just how foolish I had been, how self-absorbed, when Danielle came walking out of the bathroom. She hadn't wanted to bother me because I was so upset. She had tried to brush her own hair. Problem was, she had grabbed a round hairbrush and gotten it caught in her beautiful, long blonde hair. But that's not all…

She dealt with *that* on her own, too…because I was upset. She had gotten scissors and cut it out.

Ever think you are a horrible parent? Ever realize it's true? That was my moment. My heart was all wound up in the wrong thing that I had completely ignored my children's needs. I was broken. I apologized, hugged them both and cried more.

The bus was coming, so we fixed it the best we could. After school I cut her hair short and evened it up. I spent months looking at her hair and remembering what a terrible mother I had been that day. It was a good reminder to keep my priorities straight.

BTW...the crayon came out, but the lesson stayed with me.

Mommy, you got this!!

Mommy Moment...

I have had scary moments, but this was different.

I was pregnant with Jenna. I had a wonderful Doctor, a big jolly guy. Just a couple of months into the pregnancy I noticed a bump in my neck. At seventeen I had a similar one removed, so I knew it was my thyroid. Doc said not to worry. Sometimes the thyroid enlarges during pregnancy. I trusted him. Months later, he was out of the office one day when I had my monthly check up. I had to see another Doctor. She put me into a panic.

She saw the bump. She started saying it could be cancer and I needed tests right away. She said I may have put the baby in danger. She said if I didn't immediately have the tests, I was going to lose the baby. She said the baby might be deformed in some way already. She said she would schedule the tests right away. I wanted to wait to see my own Doctor, but she said that wasn't wise. I cried all the way home.

At home I had two young children and a husband to look after, so I got my act together and played the tough girl. When everyone was asleep...I cried some more.

I can't really explain my feelings well. I knew God was in control. I knew He was with me, yet every word that the Doctor said made my heart race and my emotions run wild. I couldn't really hear God through my own thoughts. I couldn't really trust Him. I felt I HAD to have the tests. The Doctor said so.

I remember driving to our hospital where the tests were to take place. I remember my sweaty palms on the steering wheel. I remember my heart racing.

I got to the hospital, walked into the Lab. And something snapped inside of me. It was like a part of me that had been "switched off" was suddenly "switched on". I looked at the lab tech and calmly said, "I can't do this today."

He was pompous and full of himself. "You will still have to pay for the test. This was special ordered."

I said calmly but firmly, "Fine. I will be happy to, but I'm NOT having the test today." I spun around and marched right out of the hospital. Don't try to bully me!

I don't remember ever paying for that test or even receiving a bill. But I remember clearly the freedom and relief that flooded my heart, mind and soul as I opened the door to the parking lot. I felt lighter and not fearful.

When I got home, Curt asked me what I was going to do now. I made an appointment with my own Doctor. Eventually, I did have to do more tests, but I didn't act out of overwhelming, oppressive fear.

Talk to God as if He were your best friend. Give Him all your worry and concern. Then listen. He wants to walk with you through this life. He even said so. "Draw near to Him and He will draw near to you."

Mommy, you got this!!!

Mommy Moment...

The summer Devin was a year old, my sister needed some alfalfa bales for her horses. Curt decided that it made sense to load them onto the pickup from the field rather than wait and take them from the haystack. Sounds reasonable, right?

No. That is a difficult thing to do. Well…it's difficult when you have to work with a "city girl" and have a 4-year-old drive the pickup through the field!!

Oh, yes. That is what we did. You may think we were wrong to trust a 4-year-old to drive. We may have been, but she understood and listened well.

Curt drove us all to the field. He patiently taught Danielle how to steer the pickup near the bales, but straight through the field. She had pretended to drive with Daddy many times. She understood how to keep it driving in a straight line. Devin was in his car seat beside her. Curt and I got out and walked along beside them as she drove. The pickup had a high idle, so it kept moving, even though she couldn't reach the gas pedal. When we came to a bale one of us would heft it up into the bed. Curt did more of the hefting. I eventually jumped up and stacked the bales in some sort of order. At the end of the field, Curt would jump into the driver's seat with Danielle, turn it around and line it up with the next row of bales. Off we'd go again.

Farm kids learn to work hard and listen well…at really young ages. Obedience isn't optional. Sometimes they need to listen to get work done. Sometimes they need to obey for safety reasons. On the farm, there are many dangers, and there are also many blessings. Our kids really were good kids. They understood that if Dad said do this now. He meant NOW. I wish everyone could see the value in intentionally teaching kids to obey the first time. The peace, trust and self-assuredness that comes as a result would bless many mothers.

Mommy, you got this!!

Mommy Moment...

I absolutely loved helping Curt on the farm. I was completely ignorant, but I loved doing it! He was always laughing at my interpretation of whatever he told me to do. It didn't matter what the job was, I had some bazaar way of doing it.

When we were first married Curt, his dad, and his brother were raising beef cows. That changed in the following years to dairy heifers, but in those early years their operation was simple and a bit "old school". They farmed enough ground to raise the feed for their cows. They did have large tractors, but nothing like the farm has now. The evening feeding was done with an old tractor and a wooden wagon. The wagon was loaded by hand with small hay bales, three-foot-long ones. You know the ones. They are the bales you see them use in movies to feed horses or sit on at a farm.

The year I was pregnant with Devin it was Curt and I doing evening chores. His brother wasn't home. Dad wasn't able to climb up in the haystack anymore. That left Curt… and me. We hauled 2-year-old Danielle along with us. She loved riding with Daddy!

Eight + months pregnant is NOT the time to be climbing up haystacks. Let me tell ya! But there is no way I could load them on the wagon two rows, two high, the full length of the wagon, so…

The climb up was sketchy. Once I was up on top it wasn't too bad. My balance isn't the greatest to begin with. Having a 30 pound "basketball" under my shirt really threw me off! I sat down on the top row and used my feet to push the bales down to the wagon. As I cleared one row I'd skootch down to the next lower row and do the same. It truly wasn't all that hard.

Curt thought I looked ridiculous, for sure. We laughed and just enjoyed working together. Danielle waited on the tractor, pretending to drive.

Then Dad came by. Oh, he was mad! What was a pregnant woman doing up there?! He wasn't mad and Curt or me, but I know that my brother-in-law got an earful when he returned home.

You never know what you are capable of until you try. Throwing bales was new to me, but it was good fun.

Mommy, you got this!!

Mommy Moment...

God always wants our best. We may not always know what that is, but if we learn to listen for His voice and listen to what HE says, He will guide us.

Our family enjoys going to Garage Sales and Estate Sales. It's fun to see what bargains we can find. One such day, we were out and about having a great time going around town to different Garage Sales. At one Garage Sale there was a lovely dinner table. It could seat 10 people! I really liked it, but it cost $250!! Our budget was way too tight for that, but I felt like I should buy it. What a strange thought!! I didn't NEED a table. Mine was fine it had been my sister's. It had served us well for twenty years, but our oldest daughter was married now and had 4 kids. It was a tight squeeze when we all got together at Holidays, but that only happened a few times each year. I thought about the table some more and said a quick prayer.

I wasn't sure if I heard right. Could God really want me to spend that much on something I didn't NEED? Instead of just buying it, I asked if they would call me if it didn't sell. My though was that if God really wanted me to have it then the table would not sell, and they would call, so I left my number.

I thought about the table for the rest of the day. I kept hoping they would call.

They didn't.

Maybe I was wrong. I must not have heard God's voice.

But they *did* call the next day, and the price was less!! We went right down and bought the table.

Here's the thing, it turns out I did NEED that very table. Our son-in-law got out of the Navy that November. They needed a place to live for a while as they found work here in our area. They lived with us for several months. My old table would have been way too small for all of us to sit together for meals.

God knows what we need way before we do. We just need to learn to hear His voice and do what He says. It's not always easy to know if it's His voice we hear. He understands and is so patient with us. Practice listening for Him, Sweet Mommy. He will speak you.

Mommy, you got this!!

Mommy Moment...

Whose brilliant idea was THAT?!

That's all I could think to say. There were my younger three, and several of their friends riding Caleb's little Power Wheels 4-wheeler down our hill.

Let me explain...

We live on a hill. If our house were to be built today, I imagine that it would be a 2 story with a walk out basement. Instead, it is a traditional house with a basement. They hauled truckloads of dirt onto the east side of the property to make it yard and driveway. That means we have a pretty steep drop out front on that east side. (It's the hill that Devin and his friend were sledding down, if you've read that story) There is a field road off to the north of the driveway. That part of the hill is not terribly steep and the one normally used to ride bikes and drive the little cars up and down.

This day the teens in the group had the brilliant thought to ride down the steep hill. The ride down was THRILLING! Then they had the challenge of getting the 4-wheeler back UP that hill. But, oh, they worked that out as well. They tied a rope to the undercarriage and could then haul it up without too much trouble. So, down went the rider. I don't know who the brave one to try it first was, they never told me. They all had a marvelous time! At some point, the oldest one of them started jerking on the rope before the rider got to the bottom...quite an abrupt stop! They all loved it!

More squeals of delight from the crowd!! No one was hurt. No one died. They have lovely memories of it.

Me? I was traumatized. I'm over it now. It took YEARS!! Lol.

We did have the sheriff stop a few days later. He noticed the little 4-wheeler at the bottom of the steep side of the hill. He was concerned that a child might have ACCIDENTALLY ridden off that side and be laying there hurt.

There are times, Sweet Mommies, when it's good for your kids to do things that are a bit dangerous. Especially BOYS have to be daring and just a little scary. Boys must be allowed to become men. That means that mommies must step back, take a breath and pray! I know it's hard, and there are so many ways to rationalize stepping in. I encourage you to help them figure out personal boundaries by allowing personal consequences.

Mommy, you got this!!

Mommy Moment...

I buy honey once a year from a beekeeper. I usually get 5 gallons. Yeah. I am that kind of cook. I like to purchase it locally and we truly use 5 gallons in a year…sometimes even more.

I cook with honey quite often. I started using it when I realized just how bad sugar is for you and how our kids, especially the boys, reacted to having sugary treats. (Yes, I do know that honey is still sugar.) I have found that it works in most dishes as a fair replacement for sugar. I also use it if we have a cold or sore throat to sooth our throats and kill any bad bacteria there. Did you know that honey can be used on wounds to kill bacteria? It doesn't allow bacteria to grow. It can be kept indefinitely and is still good if it crystalizes. Honey is pretty cool!

Well, unless you are trying to warm it and ...umm... totally forget about it, and ...umm... leave it on the stove all afternoon. Not cool. Not cool at all! And honey expands as it heats. Not always cool either.

I keep a small jar for honey on my counter. (A 5-gallon bucket MIGHT be a bit obnoxious on the counter. LOL.) We add it to tea or spread it on toast from that little jar. Every so often I have to take my cute little jar down to my pantry and refill it from the large bucket. Last spring, I had refilled the jar and was heating it "just a little" to help it settle in the jar and be a bit smoother to spread. But...it was spring. I looked outside. It was so sunny and warm out there. Hmmm...I will just run out for a bit and pull a few weeds.

SQUIRREL!! --My attention span is about that long.

I was happily working in the flowerbed when Kali came out and spoiled my fun. "Mom. Did you forget the honey?" Oh, no!

That was the day I learned that honey would expand at certain temperatures.

It was all over my glass top stove! I mean ALL OVER. Right to the brim! Thankfully, Kali had walked through the kitchen at that time. It probably would have run over and down the sides if she had not.

What a mess to clean up! Our hands and arms were STICKY by the time we finished. Yes, We. Kali stayed to help me, brave girl.

As you've been reading here, our household isn't exactly normal. I'm ok with that. I have a kitchen towel that reads...Remember, as far as anyone else knows we are a nice, normal family. It fits us.

Your family may not be a quirky as ours, but it's still quirky and that's ok... "NORMAL" is way overrated.

Mommy, you got this!!

Mommy Moment...

Around here, I had to make a rule about playing outside in the water. The temperature outside had to hit 80 for 3 days in a row, before they could play in the hose, put up the little pool, or set up the slip-n-slide. It may seem ridiculous to have a rule about it, but our kids were outside nearly every day. If it was nice for one day - even in JANUARY- they were ready to play in the water. They simply LOVED to do so! Having the rule stopped any argument, begging or grumbling.

It was a rule. They knew the rule. They learned to track temperatures. They learned to read several types of thermometers. They also learned patience and self-governing. Having non-negotiable rules in place helped to keep our home peaceful.

Here is another example. They were not allowed to ask for a friend to spend the night at the spur-of-the-moment. Friends were always welcome, but it had to be planned ahead of time. Begging and whining in front of the friend's parents was always going to get a negative answer. For instance, if we invited a family or two over for dinner, our kids knew that the friend could not stay unless they had asked BEFORE the families got to our home. Many friends tried the begging or teary pleas, but our kids knew the answer would be no. No emotional fuss, just simply, "We have a rule about that, so I must say no." This was nice for another reason. If our kids didn't want the other children to spend the night, they had the safely of the rule to fall back on.

The same idea applied to schoolwork. Our academic work was to begin at 7 am. The rule was they all started at 7:00 with the most difficult subject and finished with the one they liked the best, most of them ended with reading. (They love good books!) Once it was all complete, they could go have free time. No whining or they'd get an extra assignment, simple and straightforward. It worked well MOST of the time. We did have rough days occasionally.

As the kids grew, there was more wiggle room, of course. If they could explain why the rule should not apply, then I'd give in. If they pushed too hard or became emotional, we went right back to the rules. Their emotional maturity determined how I would respond.

There were many such rules.

Each family has to determine their own, but I can testify that it sure makes life more pleasant when everyone knows the rules and the rules are applied.

I'm praying for you always.

Mommy, you got this!!

Mommy Moment...

Some people might call us rednecks...

Curt and Caleb are grading our driveway. Nothing special in that. But they are pulling an antique, once horse-drawn road grader with a modern tractor up and down our driveway.

We've had that old grader for years. It belonged to Curt's Dad and his Granddad before that. That old road grader is over 100 years old! It would've been pulled by horses when Granddad had it. I think it's awesome! What a precious heirloom!

It makes me think...What am I passing down to my kids and grandkids? What will they treasure that used to be mine? A teapot? The ornaments I paint? I pray that it's more than that.

My faith in Jesus is what I pray for them to have as my legacy. I hope that the way I live shows them the truth of God's love. I hope the things I say tell them the story of God's loving sacrifice. And I hope my actions teach them they are precious, they are loved by God, and they are called by Him to do great things for His Kingdom.

Of course, I want the girls to love my tea sets and sparkly jewelry, but I pray that those things aren't the only legacy I leave them.

Mommy, you got this!!

Mommy Moment...

We had been married 17 years or so and never been on a vacation. Oh, we had gone to the mountains for a day or two at a time, sure. I mean vacation! Where you go somewhere new, see fun sights and do touristy things. Not that I minded. We had a great life. But... The thought of a REAL vacation was overwhelming!

An opportunity came for Curt and I to travel around Germany for TWO weeks because our farm purchased a Claas harvester. Curt and I would only have to pay for my ticket over. Woop! Woop! I was SO VERY excited.

Well, for a moment I was. Then the reality of leaving our five kids set in. Dani was in high school. She wasn't being home schooled, so she wouldn't be home to help with the littles except on weekends. Devin was in Jr. High here at the house, but not excited about watching and caring for three littles for that long. Then there were the little girls. They needed lots of attention and care. And, of course, Caleb who was just out of diapers and into everything. How could I even think about leaving them? What a terrible mother I was!

I prayed. I told God I just couldn't go. They were too young. It was too much for the older two. He would have to do something if He wanted us to go.

God had a plan. And it was Amazing!

First, a friend of Dani's was in college here at the community college. She said she would stay at the house. That helped, but her classes kept her super busy several days each week. I was still worried.

Then God stepped in. Just weeks before we were to leave, the High School was found to have asbestos. School officials put together a plan to share the middle school. Middle school kids had classes every other day, and the high school kids used the building on the opposite days. Dani would be home all but 5 days of our trip! Our friend could cover those few days!

I'm still in awe of how God heard my prayers and eased my mind. He must have thought I REALLY needed a vacation!

God loves us and hears us. He wants to hear from you. Nothing is too big or too small.

Mommy, you got this!!

Mommy Moment...

Homeschooling was quite a challenge for me. I struggled with feeling inadequate each and every year.

Having said that, I also absolutely loved it most days! I enjoyed being with the kids as they learned new things. My favorite part was teaching each one of them to read. I love watching their faces as they sounded out the letters, slowly at first, then, more and more fluently. There comes a day when suddenly it all makes sense to them. The letters aren't just individual sounds. The letters become words! I love that moment!

Most of the kids were 5 or 6 years old when that moment came. Kali was only 4 and Caleb was 8. Age doesn't matter. The moment it makes sense is still such a delight!

Being a good mommy is a bit like that. For some it's simple and in the natural flow of life. Others have to try a bit more. Some of us struggle a while and cry a lot. The moment we actually get it, and it all makes sense, is so thrilling!

Don't give up girls. I know you can be a great mommy! Keep trying. Look for help if you need it. There are great resources out there to help you. Ask someone you trust to mentor you. And, girls, always pray. God will help you. He will bring the people into your life to lift you up and encourage you.

Mommy, you got this!!

Mommy Moment...

When you are in the midst of raising your family it's hard to see how you could ever miss the endless work, emotional stress, dirty dishes and even dirty laundry. And yet, you will.

I, too, had so many days when I felt I'd never have a minute to myself, a minute to enjoy a clean house before five kids come in from helping Dad and track their muddy feet all across the freshly cleaned floor, a moment of peace when I didn't have to answer "Why?" for the 30th time in a day, a moment of quiet, free from the loud rowdy voices.

It may seem like a dream to think your floor will stay clean for weeks, when you won't have someone question you all day, when the only voices you have to silence are the ones in your mind. I'm not quite there yet, but I see that time drawing far too close.

I would encourage you to embrace this time you have with your littles. Dance more, the floor will wait. Answer their questions while you hold them in your lap. Join in the loud and rowdy games… use them to get the kids to clean the house. Play silly games, giggle and laugh together. Your floor will wait. The littles in your life won't. They grow each and every day.

Our home was never a show home. It was a messy home filled with messy people. The dishes weren't always done. The laundry sat in the dryer or on the couch far too many days. And the front entry was almost always covered in sand, mud and shoes of all sizes. But I loved it! I loved the mess because it was proof that our home was filled with people… the people that I dearly love. I enjoy a clean house and we usually cleaned the whole place once a week, but it never stayed clean for long. Just like at your house, about the time I thought the cleaning was finished someone came alone and made a mess.

Embrace the season you are in. They quickly pass.

Mommy, you got this!!

Mommy Moment...

Palm Sunday is special to those who follow Jesus. It's the day we celebrate Jesus coming into Jerusalem as it was prophesied. On that day he rode into the city on a donkey.

I don't know if you've ever been around donkeys, but they can have a mind of their own. All those stories of stubborn donkeys are true!

We had one on the farm. It was Curt's eldest brother's donkey. Jasper was a hoot. We loved him...right up till we were so aggravated at him that we couldn't stand him. Our feelings toward Jasper vacillated between love and hate in a moment if we were trying to work with him.

We used that little donkey to reenact Palm Sunday at our church for several years. We used him for nativity scenes as well.

Truly, he was a good little donkey. Dani and Devin would get him out as often as they could. He was great fun. They rode him all around. But, if they got off for any reason, and didn't pay really close attention, he would trot ahead and not let them back on. He stayed right close by. He didn't run off. He'd stay just far enough ahead of them that they couldn't get back on him. They'd get so aggravated at him!

But they'd be back down at his pen getting him out to ride the very next chance they got.

They have some sweet memories of that old donkey.

Our little donkey makes me wonder about the story of Christ. I'm sure the donkey he rode was just as stubborn and ornery as any other. Yet, Jesus chose him and trusted him. It gives me hope. I know I can be stubborn and ornery, too. Maybe, there's a chance that Jesus will use me and trust me… even though He knows I am that way. Maybe, I can be a bit like that donkey and serve Him… even if I am a mess.

Mommy, you got this!!

Mommy Moment…

When you are in the middle of potty-training and trying to keep track of toddlers it's hard to see far enough ahead to picture them as adults. I'm here, with adult kids, and I can tell you it's AWESOME! They are amazing people and I quite enjoy them all. They bless me in many ways!

One specific way was on my 50th birthday. I didn't think we'd celebrate it in any way, but the girls had other plans. Two things stand out about the day.

It was a Sunday; Kali had said she was going to another church and wouldn't be with us. Odd. But she is a grown up, so I didn't think much of it. But, after church when she came walking into the house, the very first thing she did was confess.

The poor girl nearly exploded…"Mom, I lied! I didn't know what else to do. I wasn't at the other church. I was getting things for your birthday party!"

What 20-year-old would be that worried about a lie to cover up a surprise party? Sweet girl! It truly upset her to have lied to me.

The other thing that stands out was the cake they ordered. It was decorated with a math equation. Basically, it said I didn't act, or look my age. Which is only half true, I'm happy to say I don't act my age…. Looks 22 + Feels 18 + Acts 10 = She's 50

They made me feel special. I love having them all home together!

Sweet Mommy, raise your kids well. Train them intentionally. Love them unconditionally. They make some of the very best friends you will ever have.

Mommy, you got this!!

Mommy Moment…

I'm sure you have days where you question why God entrusted you with kids. Or is that just me? I wondered that about myself a whole lot of days!

You know, I had busy kids. They weren't rough or disrespectful. They were just busy, always curious about the world around them, always trying to figure things out.

My mom had taught them to climb out of their cribs well before they were a year old, so by the time they were two they were very adept at climbing. Devin was the best climber of our five.

At two, he would climb up his 5-drawer dresser and sit on the top of it! Usually, he would squeal, or squawk and I'd go running into his room. There is find him, happy as a lark, sitting up there. Some days it didn't work so well. I hear a horrible thud, and sudden crying. Off I'd run, only to find him and the dresser drawers in a heap. He did it so often; I recognized the particular sound of it crashing down. He was determined to climb it, so I emptied the top two drawers. That way all the weight was in the bottom, and it was more stable.

He was never injured, but I think my heart stopped beating several times.

That kid loved daring, dangerous things. I thought I'd lose my mind. I tried explaining danger to him. I tried punishments. I tried ignoring it. Then God reminded me of several things: that daring adult men make great leaders, that being fearless is an amazing trait, and that being persistent is a great trait in a man.

When your kids are little sometimes you need to pause a minute before allowing frustration to take over. It may be that the very trait that is frustrating you might be the very trait that God is developing in them... on purpose.

I didn't always know what I was doing as a mommy, but I knew God trusted me. I had to learn to see the kids from HIS point of view. Then some of their antics weren't so distressing to my heart.

Take care, Sweet Mommy. They are only your little ones for a little while.

Mommy, you got this!!

Mommy Moment...

I believe in letting boys be boys. (I am aware that some folks disagree with that or misinterpret that saying) In our home, boys were allowed to be themselves. The boys played a little harder, a little rougher, but they were never allowed to get out of control. That didn't stop the boys from racing through the house, chasing their sisters around the house with nerf guns, or putting those poppers that you get for the Fourth of July under my car's tires to startle me as I backed the car out.

Devin and a friend had come back from the farm to ask if they could take the .22 out. They had been driving around in the little mail jeep that we owned.

Nope.

But, Mom, I know how to use it. We'll be safe.

No.

But, Mom, why not?

I said no. You know the rules.

This discussion wasn't going the way they had hoped. I knew Devin was perfectly safe and very responsible with his firearm. He was well trained. I also knew that having 2 boys together somehow divides their intelligence and multiplies their risky behavior. So, no, no firearms with friends and no adult. End of story.

Well, Devin got mad…real mad. -- Which kind of proved my point -- And he went storming back out to the jeep with his friend in tow. In his anger he hadn't noticed that my mom had pulled in. She was coming in the front door as the boys went out through the garage. He also didn't notice that she parked her brand-new car behind the jeep.

The terrible sound of metal crunching metal was the next sound we heard.

Yep. He had backed right into her car…smooshed the front fender and door.

A very calm and repentant boy returned to the kitchen. He apologized. Mom wasn't mad at all.

Well. She wasn't mad at him. She was quite mad at me. I had told him he would have to pay to have it fixed. Mom didn't think a 12-year-old boy should have to do that, especially when the insurance would cover it. Eventually, she and I compromised. He **did** pay for the damage; all of it. But, when the insurance money came in, she was allowed to deposit the check into his bank account, with the agreement that she NOT tell him about it.

It was a hard, but good lesson. The natural consequence of his anger taught him to control his temper. And, having to pay for damages helped him remember to always pay attention when he was driving.

He is a very good driver now.

It's hard to allow natural consequences to happen in your kids' lives. As a mommy we want to step in and fix it. Sometimes the hard lesson is the one that teaches them the most.

Mommy, you got this!!

Mommy Moment...

I don't know what you do for Easter, but I often end up cooking for a crowd. If you cook for 8 or 10 and think that's a crowd, imagine cooking for 200. --It boggles the mind.

I love cooking for my family. I've done Holiday meals for my family for YEARS. When Mom was still alive, I took over that roll to lighten her load. Therefore, cooking church meals came as the next step. I've served a lot of those over the years, and quite enjoy it. Not too many years ago I was put in charge of Easter Breakfast for our current church.

I had my plan. I had a list; I even had help to go shopping for supplies... Curt and Devin. Devin was home for a bit and volunteered to go get supplies at Sam's with Curt and me. I love having help!!

We decided to take our Explorer. Good thing, too, because we didn't come home with just groceries!

I don't know if you have any idea how big the Explorer's cargo area is, but it's pretty big. You flip the two back seats, and you can stack a LOT of groceries in there! I know because we did. Food for 200? No big deal.

Curt had heard of a pawn shop near Sam's and we all thought it sounded like fun. So, off we went. Wow! They had some screaming good deals! One in particular caught Curt's eye. They had a full set of Carol Shelby tires and rims that fit Curt's car... at a quarter of their value!

Ok. If that sounds like a foreign language, let me put it this way...Curt owns a Shelby Mustang (super-fast, super-hot car) this shop had four wheels that were especially made for THAT car. AWESOME!

Well, sort of awesome. We had no room, remember? We had groceries for two hundred people in the car. There was no space for those four wheels. Not awesome.

Curt said he'd just come back another day for them. I was worried that someone else would buy them before he would have another free day and the time to go get them.

No worries. As a mommy I have honed my SUPER TETRAS skills. You girls have, too. You play TETRAS when you load the dishwasher. You play TETRAS when you put away Christmas decorations. You play

TETRAS when you stow away summer games and toys. Mommies are great finders of extra room to tuck things into, right?

I am happy to say, I made room for those wheels in the back of that car. I had to stash those groceries into the back seat clear to the roof. I think Devin thought I was going to leave HIM at the pawn shop.

No. I didn't leave him, but I did have him hold some groceries on his lap. I had some, too. But...Curt got his fancy wheels!

Mommy, you just never know when the skills you've learned as a mother will come in super handy.

Mommy, you got this!!

Mommy Moment...

All mommies have stories of how their children came to them. Some have birth stories. Others have adoption stories. But we all have stories. Mine are unusual...like everything else in my world.

We attended "Prenatal Classes" when we were expecting our first. That's what pregnant couples did back them. They taught me how to "Breathe". They told me there would be a time I'd be told to "push". They warned me about "Braxton Hicks" contractions. They did NOT prepare me for my first birth experience.

Curt, one of his friends, and I were out playing Frisbee Sunday afternoon. It was a beautiful, warm day for the end of February. I was struggling to catch the Frisbee. My stomach kept tightening all weird, and my balance was all off. It didn't hurt, but it sure made it tough to catch that thing. Curt made fun of me. I finally gave up. I was just off my game.

Monday, I was busy... quite busy. I cleaned the whole house (all 600 square feet) I cooked a nice meal. I was all ready for Curt when he got home from the farm. We had plans to go over to the hospital about 7 pm and pre-register (something you did 40 years ago). It meant we were about two weeks from having our baby! --I was so excited and ready.

We went over after dinner. We were given a short tour and then we had some forms to fill out. The nurse was just a little rude. She kept staring at me. When I'd catch her at it, she'd look away. It was getting on my nerves.

"Honey, how long have you been having contractions?" she finally asked.

"Well. I've been having "Braxton Hicks" contractions for DAYS!"

Her eyes got big, "They're pretty close together."

"Yeah. They've been like that all day."

I think she nearly fainted. "How about I check you before you go home? They are about 2 minutes apart."

"Ok. Whatever, but they've been like this all day. I'm not due for 17 days."

Sure enough. She was right. I was in full labor! If she had left me alone, I probably would've had the baby at home. As it was, she made me lay down and hooked me up to their monitors.

Laying down made my back ache! I kept running the bed up and down. I had Curt rubbing my back. Nothing helped. After an hour or so I made a fuss and got the nurse to unhook me, so I could walk around a bit.

Yep! That's what I needed. I got as far as the door and grabbed the doorjamb. The baby rolled over. My stomach did the wave. Suddenly, we were in business! About 20 minutes later we had our sweet baby girl in our arms! It was a little after 10 pm…and 17 days before we had expected.

God made sure we were at the hospital at just the right time. I wasn't smart enough to realize that the contractions I'd been having for the past 24 hours weren't false contractions. Those were REAL ones!

He has His hands full trying to keep me out of trouble.

Mommy, you got this!!

Mommy Moment…

My appointment was the last one before lunch that Friday. My mom had offered to keep Danielle with her, so I didn't have to take her with me. It's a good thing she did.

The doctor was running late and a little bit frantic. I made it worse.

You are dilated to 6!! You must go straight to the hospital!

Ok, but first I need to run home and get Curt.

No. You need to hurry right over. You are in labor!

I listened politely, and… went home to get Curt.

Well...my friend lived halfway between town and our house, so... I stopped to tell her that I was in labor and about to have the baby.

I was so excited! I could hardly sit still to drive.

Once I made it home, Curt had to have lunch...and a shower. He is always calm and levelheaded. He told me to lay down and rest while he took his shower. Can you imagine!

Yes. We knew I was in labor. Yes. We knew I was getting closer and closer to delivering.

Once we were ready, we loaded up my overnight bag and were finally on the way to the hospital. It was 2:20 when we were about halfway to town. I know because I happened to look at the clock, and I thought with a smile, "So much for hurrying right over to the hospital."

We parked. I had to pause for a second as I got out of the car. We walked up to the front steps. Again, I had to stop and take a deep breath. Curt teased me a little, asking if I needed a wheelchair.

When we walked into the OB ward, the nurse fussed a bit. (Another contraction) They had been expecting me, but they had two other ladies in delivery. I'd have to wait in a regular room.

Wait!!?? Are you kidding! (Another contraction)

Remember, I was young, only 21. The nurse was sure I had no clue about labor. I'm sure she thought I would be in for hours before I had the baby. I had to argue with her just a bit. "At least, check me. Check me before you leave the room," I requested. (Another contraction)

As soon as she did, she changed her tune! "You're in labor!!! The baby's almost here!"

I'm sure I rolled my eyes. Devin was clocked in at 2:43.

I'm so glad God knew I needed my appointment on that very day. Otherwise, Curt might have been delivering a baby during his lunch break.

Mommy, you got this!!

Mommy Moment...

When will I learn?! I thought I was all grown up and passed the age of doing ridiculous things... apparently not.

I was happily making supper just now. I wanted to make a spinach dip as a part of it. That should be easy enough, right? It only has 5 ingredients and I have all of them on hand. Woohoo!

I was allowing the frozen spinach to thaw before squeezing out the liquid and adding it. I had everything else in the bowl. I thought I'd give it a quick stir and let it rest. My "quick stir" may have been a just bit too enthusiastic. A good sized 'glop' shot up and landed in my right eye.

Are you done laughing?

Rightfully so. How old will I be before I stop doing such ridiculous things??!!

I imagine God smiled and shook His head as He watched me. As a mommy you will watch your kids make lots of mistakes. Some mistakes are serious and need heartfelt encouragement to get passed. Some mistakes may need disciplining. Others deserve a shake of your head and a grin, or even a belly laugh. Kids need to make mistakes, but to do that they need a safe environment where mistakes are allowed. Life is hard enough on our kids. Be sure to make your home their safe space.

Mommy, you got this!!

Mommy Moment...

Curt and I are both the youngest children in our respective families, and we both were raised more like only children because of age gaps. Therefore, we knew we didn't want Jenna to be raised alone. She needed a sibling near her age, so we were super excited about being pregnant again. My heart was cautious because of the previous miscarriages, but that was in God's hands. I prayed hard and didn't tell anyone that I was pregnant until I was a solid 5 nearly 6 months along. I also struggled with the memories of what had happened to Jenna in the hospital. I couldn't get over the thought of that happening to another child. I begged God not to make me have this baby in the hospital.

But, like any prayer, if you don't take any action you probably won't see any answer. I didn't contact a midwife, so my options were limited. I continued to pray. Although Curt had helped deliver many calves, and lambs, he had NO interest in a home birth. So... I prayed...and cried.

As the time drew nearer for Kali to be born my prayers became more fervent. She was due just after Christmas, the 30th. Our first three kids were all born early, so I expected her to be early as well. Christmas came and went. No baby. New Year's came and went. No baby. She is the only one of our five that was late. I blame my own unsettled heart for that. I TRULY did not wish to have her at the hospital.

I had been restless all night. I have contractions for months before I actually go into labor, so I'm used to focusing on my breathing and calming my heart. I knew that if I made too much noise or rolled around excessively Curt would awaken and haul me into the hospital. I laid as still as I could. I prayed as hard as I could. The contractions kept coming. At about 5 am he rolled over to me, and told me I was in labor, he was headed downstairs to wake up Danielle so she could be upstairs with Jenna, and I needed to get up and ready. We were going to the hospital!

You mommies know how emotional you are in labor. I just wanted to cry. Instead, once he dressed and left the room I got up. I started to get ready to go when suddenly, I knew we weren't going ANYWHERE!! I was not making it to the car let alone the hospital.

Curt was only gone about five minutes. His face went white when he returned to our room in time for me to say, "The baby is here. You gotta catch!!"

Yep. She was and he did. Poor guy. One good contraction and he was holding his new little daughter. She has had him wrapped around her little finger ever since.

Mommy, you got this!!

Mommy Moment...

I have told you just how upset I was when I figured out that not only was I unexpectedly pregnant. Another struggle was the fact that the baby was due on the one-year anniversary of my mom's death. Having said that, once I got over myself and my grief, I was super excited to welcome this little babe into our family.

My pregnancy had been like the others, super easy. My body LOVES being pregnant. This time Curt insisted that I find a midwife if I was determined to have the baby here at home. He wasn't in favor of being the "delivery guy."

I researched and found a lady in a city about an hour from us who had been a floor nurse, trauma nurse, OB nurse and a hospital administrator who was now a midwife. I felt sure she would know what she was doing. Yep. She sure did!

You'd think that after delivering four babies I would know what I was doing. Nope. She taught me so much. She required her clients to attend her monthly classes. I sat there with my eyes wide and my mouth hanging open at everyone. For instance, did you know that eating protein (an egg or small piece of meat) when you first awaken in the morning will cure most morning sickness? Me either. How about, thrush in your baby is a lack of heathy bacteria in the mommy? Or maybe, being active right up to birth makes delivery easier? Well, she had all the stats and had worked all sides of the OB world. It was enlightening and quite fun. I enjoyed every class and interaction with Kelly.

Anyhow…I had been having contractions… like always. But that evening just before we went to bed, I told Curt I felt funny. There wasn't anything to put my finger on, but I felt "funny." Right away he said to call Kelly, so I did. I answered her questions; No. nothing is different. No, my contractions aren't any closer. No, they aren't lasting longer. No. I don't "feel" like I'm in labor.

She said she would be right down. It's an hour drive, so she would head out right away just to check me and be safe.

Ok. I felt silly making her drive down, but I understood. She wanted to be safe because I had delivered quickly before.

We decided to go ahead and go to bed. Kelly would just come on in when she got here.

Curt called her back ten minutes after the first call to tell her... It's a BOY!!!

Again, Curt was the "delivery guy."

Mommy, you got this!!

Mommy Moment...

The day was just like any other day. The kids and I were in our "school room". We had rearranged the house, so that our front bedroom could be our school room. I thought it would help the older two do their academic work without the little 2 getting into their stuff. It helped most days. I thought they were doing schoolwork, but somehow, they were looking out the windows this particular November day.

What they noticed concerned me. There was a police car, lights flashing, driving down our road. We stopped to watch it. It turned and went toward the farmyard. A thought flooded my mind, "Curt's dream." I tried to find the words to explain to the kids what I thought might have happened…

In August, Curt had awakened from a dream one-night sweating, anxious, heart pounding. In his dream Dad had fallen in his yard and died at Curt's feet. As you can imagine, it took quite a while for Curt to relax and calm down enough to go back to sleep.

We both prayed that it was nothing more than a dream.

…After watching the first policeman, we saw another. Then an ambulance came by. It took a few minutes for Curt to call me. Curt and Dad had been working on the Corrals in the farmyard. Dad had tripped over some of the pipes they were using.

We discovered later that his neck snapped when he hit the ground.

Curt had worked nearly every day of his life with his father. He adored his father. They were business partners, co-workers, and friends. Curt had been his shadow from the time he was two or three years old. Dad was a great man!

Without the dream that Curt had months before, Curt would have been crushed by the death of his father. But God had warned him. It truly helped us deal with it all.

God was with us. He had warned us and prepared us. In his Word He promises to be with His people. He says He sends His Spirit to comfort them. The events in our lives have been at times shocking, other times distressing and some have been extraordinary, but God has been faithful and kind in good times and bad.

We may not always have a warning come in a dream, but we always have His Spirit with us. I pray that you will feel His love and comfort each and every day.

Mommy, you got this!!

Mommy Moment...

We live in the country. We have a lovely view of green fields and colorful sunrises. What we don't have is paved roads. Dirt, dirt and more dirt, that's what we have, tiny bit of sidewalk around the house, and no pavement. It makes it hard for kids to do things such as scooter, ride a bike or skateboard. Riding a bike in sand is hard enough for someone who has been riding for years, for a little guy just learning it's really tough.

Devin must have been about five. It was a lovely sunny day. He wanted to learn to ride a bike. Oh, that's not quite true. He knew HOW. He just had not done so without training wheels. Devin had been begging to have them removed, so he could REALLY ride. He talked Daddy into helping him. It was sweet to watch them work together to get the wheels off and prepare for the big moment. Daddy walked beside him and talked with him as he peddled to the top of our driveway. Daddy gave him one last bit of advice. I didn't hear the words, but he told him to swing away from the cars in front of the house.

I don't know about you, but once something is in my head, I have a difficult time NOT thinking about it. For our little guy, it was just that way.

He was worried about the cars, so that's what he was watching. Naturally, that's exactly the direction he steered.

Smack!! Right into the 66 Mustang, breaking out one of the lights.

The poor kid felt terrible!! – But he did learn to ride the bike that day. It just took a few tries.

I'm so much like that little boy. I get my focus on the wrong things. When the kids were little it was easy to begin to compare what I was doing to what I thought other moms were doing. I looked at the wrong things and didn't stay clear of the obstacles. Instead, I headed right for them.

Sweet Mommy, Hang in there. Keep your focus on the goal, the goal of training up your children. Don't look at others and compare or wish you were different. I have often said I don't fit in a box. You know… the "perfect mother box," or the "perfect Christian box," "the perfect

Homeschool mom box" even the "got it all together box". I am just me. I follow Christ the best I can. I did the best I could to be a good mommy. I strive to go the direction He asks me to go. I am willing to try. I am willing to become who God says I am. I hope you are, too. We just need to keep our focus on the right things.

Mommy, you got this!!

Mommy Moment...

Ever look back at old photos of yourself and wonder, "What was my mother thinking?!!"

I remember sitting in a chair and having Mom run a piece of tape across my forehead. I also remember the feeling of dread. In my day mothers often cut the children's hair, not always with the best results. Mom kept mine pretty short, bangs cut straight across my forehead and the rest cut just below my ears. My brothers affectionately called me a little Beatle, because my hair resembled that of the guys in The Beatles rock group. When I became old enough to have an opinion about my hair Mom took me to a cousin of hers who was a barber. THAT wasn't much better. I left the shop nearly in tears! I dreamed of hair like Valerie Bertinelli and instead, I looked like a poodle… a poodle with blind groomer.

At the wise and all-knowing age of 11 I decided that cutting my thick curly hair on my own was the way to go. I had watched Mom's cousin carefully. I could do what she did. I had been a "Beatle" and a "poodle". Surely hacking it off on my own couldn't be worse, and it might even be an improvement! That was the beginning.

I cut my own hair (with very mixed results) from then on. I still don't go in to have it professionally done often. The most of the time, I trim it myself.

Mommy, what would you do with a daughter who cut her hair? I have no idea what Mom thought. I don't remember her ever questioning me or making any comment about my hair. I assume she noticed… how could she not? I often look back at memories like this and wonder what my parents thought. I wish I could ask them.

I am positive my own children will look back in their memories and wonder what I was thinking, maybe not because of a bad haircut…then again, maybe that, too. I did cut their hair when they were growing up. I know Mom did the very best she could at the time. I know she had her reasons for doing the things she did. Her life was not easy. I'm sure having me as a "bonus" baby added all kinds of stress. I hope my kids will have that same kind of grace for me that I have for her. I certainly made a mess of things at times, but I have tried my best and tried not to make the same mistakes twice.

Your kids will also grow up and look back. Their memories are yet to be made. Laugh with your kids; teach them to look for joy. Play games with your kids; teach them there is value in having fun together. Work hard with them; learning responsibility early will take them far in life.

And, PLEASE, Sweet Mommy, don't subject them to every fad haircut or hairstyle that comes around. LOL.

Mommy, you got this!!

Mommy Moment...

You have noticed that I can be a bit "Mama Bear" when it comes to protecting my kids. Oh, I am so much more "Mama Bear" when it comes to my husband.

We had been married just over a year when I began to have an odd feeling when a friend of mine was around. No, she wasn't chasing Curt; I would have ended the friendship immediately! I just began to feel manipulated, like she was a child going between parents to get the answer she wanted. For instance, she would ask me if I would like to go to the movies. Once we had Danielle, I didn't like to leave her at night, so I would say no, and think nothing more of it. Later, when Curt was home, he would ask me if I wanted to go to that same movie. Funny, I thought.

I discovered that if I said no, she would ask Curt when I was not in the room. She'd also tell him that I really hoped to go to THAT movie. Once I caught on, I knew I would have to deal with the situation.

I knew her back story. Her parents had divorced when she was a young teen. I think that had taught her to go to both parents looking for the answer she wanted, and therefore she treated us that way as well. I don't believe she was malicious. I doubt she even realized what she was doing, but I still had to deal with it, even if I understood it.

She came out one weekend. The same scene began to play out, so I sat down beside her on our couch and began to gently explain what I saw happening. I told her that my marriage was more important than my friendship with her. Through tears, I explained that she would no longer go between us to manipulate us into doing whatever it was she wanted us to do.

Here's the deal. I had felt responsible for that girl. When her parents when through their divorce my mom had asked me to befriend her and help her. I had done that. I actually attended a few of her counseling sessions because her parents had asked me to help her sort her feelings and open up. It broke my heart to think I might have to let go of her, to walk away from the one girlfriend I had. It took every bit of courage I had to stand up for my marriage and choose to protect my relationship with Curt.

As I feared, she took offence. She chose to walk away from us. That day was the last day she was ever in our home. Having toxic friends can destroy a marriage. Girls, you can't just be protective of your sweet littles. They grow up and leave you to start their own lives. You need to be a fierce protector of your husband, not fierce AT him, fierce FOR him. Keeping your marriage as a priority will ensure your littles have the security they need and will make it easier when you become an empty nester.

I adore my hubby!! Marriage isn't easy. It is worth fighting for, I promise.

Mommy, you got this!!

Mommy Moment...

I was baking cookies with my mom in her kitchen. Four-year-old Danielle was playing in the other room. Devin was playing around at our feet. Suddenly, he leaned over and BIT the back of my calf. Ouch. Without a thought, I reached down and popped him under the chin. I surprised him as much as he surprised me!

Normally, our discipline was more thought out and intentional. In that moment, it was simply a reaction. He NEVER bit again.

I don't advise disciplining without forethought.

The things we disciplined for were disrespect of parents or anyone, and straight defiance. The list seems short, but it covered plenty of bad behaviors. The punishments were at times quite creative. Intentionally dropping food on the floor just might mean you had to get down on your hands and knees and lick it up. YUCKY! Getting loud during a church service would get you a warning look and an "air pat". If you continued your ear might get flicked. The most common consequence was just a "look" with raised eyebrows. In our home, it took serious sass, actual defiance or mean behavior to get a single swat. Rarely did any of the kids push it that far, but they knew I wasn't afraid to parent them if they choose to break the rules.

Here's the deal. I taught them to respect what I said when they were tiny. It began when I would change their diaper and needed them to lay still. I would make a disapproving sound, "aahhk" and roll them back. If they continued to roll, I would pop their bottom lightly. That's all it took. As they grew, the "look", the sound and the eyebrow raising were usually all it took to remind them that they needed to change their behavior. Kids want to please! If I was consistent with the rules, they felt safe and didn't push me.

I wasn't that way as a young mom. It took me a while to figure that out. Poor Danielle and Devin were the Guinea Pigs. I was very consistent with Danielle and began to doubt myself by the time Devin came around. Our society made me feel like I had been mean to Danielle, so I backed down. I didn't treat baby Devin the way I had baby Danielle. It set up poor Devin for failure and insecurity. It's the main thing I regret in my parenting. By the time the younger three kids came along I had realized my mistake and parented them much the same way as I had Danielle. They very rarely got into trouble.

It's well known that if I got after Jenna, even with just the "look" she would melt into a puddle of tears…and I would do the same right along with her. Kali and Caleb say they watched everyone else get into trouble and that was enough to convince them to behave well. Kali adds… Caleb still did "all the things" he just didn't get into trouble for them.

Mommy, my advice is start when they are young. Build a relationship based on truth and respect. By that I mean, tell them what you expect and tell them what the consequences will be, then hold firm. I often cried when I had to get after a child. It would break my heart, but I LOVE them enough to hold them accountable for their choices. I'm also very quick to forgive them when they are truly repentant. Be unreservedly free with your love and mercy when they are repentant.

Love them well! We are only stewards. They belong to God.

Mommy, you got this!!

Mommy Moment...

Me: The cigarette lighter is hot. Be careful with that. It gets HOT!

Danielle: ok.

Famous last words.

We were at my mom's, in her car. We had spent the day with my folks. We had driven to a nearby city just to go shopping. When we got back to Mom's, Danielle had some questions. Danielle had asked what the lighter was. I explained. I warned her that it would burn her and went inside.

That girl! She never pushed the rules; she never questioned my authority... well, almost never. That day, she pushed. That day she questioned. That day, she didn't believe me.

I went on in. We had spent a wonderful day out with my folks, but we needed to get home. I was saying my goodbyes to my folks. I don't know what got into Danielle. She pushed the lighter in, when it popped out, she promptly stuck her finger in it. The circular burn stayed there on the end of her finger for weeks! It left quite a mark! I'm surprised she still has a fingerprint on that finger.

We do what we can. We inform. We warn. We teach. At the end of the day, we have to let them choose...sometimes they choose poorly.

Dani remembers it well, the warning, the burn, and the lesson. Sweet Mommy, they may make poor choices. Will you still love them if they do? Will you still be kind?

I don't always make the right choice, but God loves me. I must extend that grace to my kids, even when it's hard.

Mommy, you got this!!

Mommy Moment...

And there was the CAT hanging onto the wall!!! Literally.

My niece and her family loved to come out from the city for visits. Sometimes they would be here for just a day or two, other times they would stay for a week. They came quite often for Spring Break. (Welcome to Aunt Shell's Bed and Breakfast. LOL) Sometimes they would bring other friends or families with them. It was delightful! Her first three kids are the ages of our younger three. They were the best of friends. When we got together it was a bit like having three sets of twins!! They could think of more stuff to get in to!!

This time the whole family was staying for several days. We were having a great time. The kids were off playing somewhere. Their dachshund was keeping an eye on everyone. She was perfectly happy running around here. I think she liked visiting the farm as much as their kids did.

We adults were laughing and visiting. Jenna's kitten came to the back door. She was mostly an outside cat, but the kids loved to have her in. They spoiled her. We were extra good to her for two reasons. One, she was a beautiful white kitty. Two, Jenna found her nearly starving and quite bedraggled at our church and had adopted her into our family and nursed her back to good health.

One of us let Miss Kitty in. She strutted into the living room, about eight feet in from the door, making sure all of us saw how pretty she was. The Dachshund came into her view. Suddenly, the cat, in one giant leap jumped up about seven feet and managed to sail toward our rock fireplace another eight feet away and to the right. I'm not kidding when I say she CLUNG to the rocks! She clung there, right at the ceiling. WOW!! I have not ever seen a cat move so fast or jump so far or fly through the air quite like that! It was pretty amazing! We had a terrible time getting her down from there.

We were all so shocked it took several seconds for any of us to react. I will never forget the poor white kitty hanging on the wall!

Life comes with surprises, both good and bad. Don't stress. Find humor in the moment.

Mommy, you got this!!

Mommy Moment...

Jenna was such a pretty little girl. I know that sounds prejudiced, but she truly was stunning. She had bright blue eyes, long blonde hair, and a lovely bronze skin tone. People would stop us when we were out to tell me how beautiful she was. They would tell me I should let her model. I even had one friend in particular who encouraged, pushed actually, me to let her be in commercials. She would tell me the dates and times to take Jenna for modeling calls in Denver.

Let me try to explain why that was never an option in my heart.

You probably have heard the stories of child stars. They become famous, the family gets rich, lives high-on-the-hog, kid gets into all sorts of trouble. Another scenario...kid gets famous, mom loves the attention and fame, she pushes the kid more and more, family disintegrates. Those are common stories of child stars.

I couldn't, wouldn't, subject my family to that. I couldn't, wouldn't, subject my daughter to that. There was something in my heart that was horrified at the thought of what might happen to the sweet, innocent little heart of Jenna. I wasn't willing to risk it. To me it wasn't worth the possible destruction of my beautiful daughter.

There will be times, Sweet Mommy, when you have the world around you pushing you to make decisions that won't sit right in your heart. Don't let them push you into something that you feel is harmful. You, not them, have been entrusted with those littles who call you Mommy. Seek God's help. Fiercely protect their hearts.

Mommy, you got this!!

Mommy Moment...

What's a mother to do? You're in the car on a long journey. The kids are good, but they are getting tired of it. They begin to ask that famous and annoying question...Are we there yet?

What do you do? How do you answer without encouraging whining?

Curt rescued me here. I would not have known what to do. He answered the question the same way no matter how far away we were from our destination. We might have just left the house or might have been ready to pull into wherever we were going. It mattered not.

"We're halfway there."

ALWAYS the same answer. "We're halfway there."

Kids are smart! It didn't take them long to realize what was going on. Instead of fussing at them or arguing with them in any way, he just stated matter-of-factly...We're halfway there.

I love the wisdom in his answer! The kids quickly learned that the question would not get a rise out of Dad. It was completely useless to try. It actually became a bit of a game. They would ask as we left the house just to tease Dad, or they'd ask and then all of them would answer in unison..."We're halfway there!"

The kids are all grown up. If you were to ask any one of them a question relating to distance, or that MIGHT be construed to relate to distance..."We're halfway there." is the answer you will get.

Mommy, you got this!!

Mommy Moment...

Where do you go to get a haircut for a 3-month-old baby boy?

Back when our first son came along I had quite a dilemma. The kid was born with more hair than most 1-year-olds have. By the time he was 3 months old he had hair nearly to his shoulders. What do you do?

I mentioned before, I cut my own hair. I even cut Curt's, but a baby!!? That was frightening to me. I could not find one hairdresser would cut his hair, but it was getting way too long. SOMEONE was going to have to cut it!

There was no way he could sit up, and he would never lay still. After much contemplating I devised a plan. After nursing him I would rock him to sleep. While he slept in my arms, I would trim off the longest bits in the back. It worked! ...well sort of.

After the first try, it looked a bit like a 2-year-old had held him down and taken scissors to it. I had to follow the plan several days before I felt like it looked good enough to take him out in public. From then on, I cut his hair. Actually, the kid was in college before anyone else cut it.

Sweet Mommy, in your motherhood journey there will be so many things that you will not want to do, things that may frighten you, or make you feel incompetent. Take a minute to assess the situation. Can someone else do it? If not, make a plan. Don't be afraid to try. Failure won't hurt. Trial and error taught me oh so many things. You can do it, Girl!

Mommy, you got this!!

Mommy Moment...

Did you ever read Tom Sawyer? Remember the part were Tom convinced the other kids to paint a fence? They gave him their "treasures" in payment so he would allow them the privilege of doing the work. Some kids are so gullible!

Yeah, well... We have our own Tom Sawyer. Sweet little Jenna. Shocking, huh?

I mentioned that my niece and her family visited regularly. Quite often they came over spring break. That happens to be the same time of year when the chicken house needs cleaned out. That was a chore assigned to our kids. It's not a hard job, but it's dusty and dirty, and certainly NOT a favored chore.

For 2 or 3 consecutive years, sweet little Jenna convinced her cousins to help clean it out. They were convinced it was FUN!

I'd look out the window and there I'd see 4 kids just working away! Jenna wasn't always with them.

Even tough jobs can be fun… if you're creative enough.

Mommy, you got this!!

Mommy Moment...

Oh, Sweet Mommy. You are hurting. You are trying your best and still feel like you are a failure. You feel like you are messing up your kids, like you are a terrible mother. You can't seem to get it all together. I know. I've been there too.

It matters not what your circumstances are. Maybe your kid fell today from the swing and broke an arm. Maybe she was drinking from the toilet. Maybe you clipped your infant's nails too short and they bled. Maybe he threw eggs all over your kitchen. We've all had those days… sometimes weeks. There will be weeks where your heart will burst from loving them so very much, and weeks where you feel you should never have become a mom.

If you have read any of my previous stories, you know that I struggled. I felt lost and incapable. What I need you to know is… feelings change, it's common, you aren't the only one, but you have the ability to change if you need to. All of us have those moments. I remember those feelings. I cried so very often. Here are a few things I did to make it through those moments.

Usually, I would go sit on my bathroom floor and cry and pray. I remember little fingers wiggling underneath the door and little voices calling for me while I sat there sobbing. I would pray there in that bathroom, sometimes silently, sometimes loudly. When the kids were a little older, I would walk around our property. It's 2 or 3 acres, one loop was usually long enough to calm my emotions. Only once did I get in my car and drive the "block" (out here that's a 5 to 10-mile loop). Here is what I learned: I am responsible for my own emotions. –Not rocket science, but extremely important. It took a while for me to realize that I get to tell my feelings truth. Feelings ebb and flow. Truth is constant. My own heart needed to be anchored to TRUTH. My relationship with God is an anchor for me, as is my husband.

God has always reminded me of His love for me …even in those moments. His tremendous love for me speaks to my heart and reminds me that I truly adore my kids. Reading God's Word, especially Psalms, shows me that I am NOT the first to love God yet struggle with emotions. Reading Acts tells me that the Holy Spirit will help me.

And then there is my husband. He is levelheaded. He allows me to cry, but it never sways his loyalty or love. He doesn't know what to do with my tears, but they never change his heart toward me.

I don't know what anchors your heart to truth. You may have a mother to call, or a friend. You may just need a hot cup of coffee or a moment of silence. Whatever it is hold on to that. Don't allow your emotions to change who you are, and don't believe the lies that emotions tell you.

I once stomped on my kitchen floor in frustration/anger. It hurt my heal so badly that I hobbled for days. I learned that sitting in the bathroom crying for a few minutes was FAR less painful and definitely more productive. Pray, Sweet Mommy! Pray for God to intervene and flip the atmosphere of your heart. He can do that. He can show you TRUTH and help you get the emotions back in check. Find TRUTH and anchor your heart to it.

Mommy, you got this!!

Mommy Moment...

Our babies slept like angels. From the time they were 3 or 4 weeks old they slept at least 8 hours at night. It wasn't always convenient times; 6pm to 2am or midnight to 8, but they slept well.

My momma was "old school" she taught me to feed them on a schedule, bathe them in the evening, then feed them while rocking them and lay them down for the night. It worked great for all 5 of ours. Now, we did have our moments when it didn't work, but overall, it was amazing!

Funny thing, at the time of our first kids, mothers were taught to give baths in the mornings. The thought was baths would wake them up and keep them awake in the daytime. Also, it was taught that you didn't want them to get hungry, so you were to feed babies whenever they wanted to eat. Mom gave me her opinion of bath time and feeding schedules and left it at that. I had to choose who to listen to, the "experts" or my mom. I chose my mom.

I made the mistake of listening to the "experts" when it came to potty-training. Wait till they're older, they said. Wait till they can take themselves, they said. They should be at least two, they said. Yeah, I tried that twice. Both times were rough. Mom kept saying, train them early, before they have their own opinions of things. Start just before they're a year. My last three were much easier to train.

You all know that developmentally kids around two suddenly realize they have opinions, likes and dislikes. Trying to potty-train at that point in development didn't work well for me. I would get so frustrated. The kids would get so frustrated. It was awful! With the younger three, I went with Moms opinion. Guess what? It was so much easier! We began at 10 months old or so...just like Mom said.

I have had to make that same choice oh so many times! Who do I listen to? On everything from treating fevers to potty-training, there are "experts" in every generation. I like to hear various opinions. But, for me, the best advice came from older mommies who had four, five or even six kids. Those ladies lived it. And, they had learned from the generation before them, not from a book.

Somewhere along the way, we as a society decided that "experts" were the ones with college degrees not the ones with experience. I would encourage you to sit and visit with your Grandma or mom. Listen to the wisdom they have to share. They may not be "experts," but their words of wisdom are worth listening to, even if you make a different choice.

Mommy, you got this!!

Mommy Moment...

Do you remember the day you met the people who would eventually be your in-laws? How did that go? Here is how we met one of our now sons-in-law...

Colton first met us at church. He attended the same church as Danielle and Jeff. Jeff and Colton were on the worship team together, so they'd known each other for a couple years. He knew Danielle, too. She was the nice lady who served the coffee and donuts sometimes. Apparently, after seeing Jeff with Dani and their kids, and realizing those two were married, he said, "Wow! How did He get HER?! And... does she have a sister?!"

Well, yes. Yes, she does, 2 actually. One of them was attending that very same church, but he hadn't noticed... not until one day after church.

I remember the day Colton realized that Danielle had a sister. We were up visiting Jenna that weekend and had decided to go to church as one big happy family. We, 15 of us counting children, were gathered together after church trying to make a plan for lunch. It was taking us quite a while to make a decision. Danielle and Jeff were standing together at the edge of our crowd. Colton came up and stood beside them. He said NOTHING. This stranger just stood there listening to our conversation. I thought it strange. I wondered why he stayed there but didn't speak to us. He stayed right there by Jeff until we all began to leave the building.

Apparently, after we left, he asked Jeff if he could have Jenna's name and number. Jeff obliged him.

Danielle sent Jenna a text telling her of what Jeff had done and warning her that Colton, the cellist from church, might call her. Good thing she warned Jenna. He sent a text to Jenna that very afternoon! That was the beginning of their love story.

In his version of this story, Colton adds that Curt and I look like Gargoyles guarding the beautiful princess.

I think that means he called his mother-in-law a mid-evil, creepy animal, but I'm not sure. LOL

Mommy, you got this!!

Mommy Moment...

I remember the awkward age in between being a child and being an adult. You feel like you are more grown up than you are, but you don't like to be left out of the fun of childhood. For the last 10 or 15 years we have hosted a flashlight Easter egg hunt for our kids, their friends, and even random neighbor kids. When we started this tradition, it was because I felt like our teens were too old to hunt eggs and too young not to want to.

Curt and I hide the eggs, somewhere around 1000 of them. We have 15 or 20 teenagers with flashlights wandering around our property in the dark. They fill our house with laughter as they fill their bags with eggs. It's so much fun!!

This year, all our babies are grown, the youngest in over 21. Yet…Here I am, stuffing hundreds of eggs in preparation for our flashlight Easter-Egg hunt. I have bags of candies and small toys all around the front room. It's a disaster around here! Seven tall kitchen trash bags of eggs!!

You know what? Even if they tell me one year that they are too old for such silliness, I think I will still host one anyway. I absolutely LOVE hosting. I spend hours searching for silly toys and candies. I try to find things that will make them happy. The anticipation I feel at the thought of a house full of young adults and teens thrills my heart. Watching the beams from their flashlights bob all around our yard while I listen to them giggle makes me smile. And, the moment when they have their eggs and they gather back in the house going through their stash is a blast. The balloons get blown up and chased around the house by ADULTS with plastic "sticky hands." The small flying monkeys are shot all around. The sound of Slap Bracelets snapping is continuous. They are just as excited as small children on Christmas morning. It is a highlight of my year.

Sweet Mommy, it's good to be childlike, the pure joy and excitement, the innocent heart. It's ok to find happiness in simple things.

Mommy, you got this!!

Mommy Moment...

How do you feel when a child tattletales? I was raised as an only child. I had no idea if it was normal or not. If it is normal, how much is too much? Is it ok for a mommy to rely on that? Hmmm...

Tough call. Here is my take and why...

One of my goals as a mommy was for my kids to be friends, not only as littles, but as adults, too. I worked hard to find ways to encourage that. I also tried to watch for things that came between them. When a child is allowed to tell a trusted adult something, knowing that another child will get punished, it does several things. One, it breaks the bond and the trust between the two kids. Two, it gives power or control to a child. Three, it undermines the authority of the adult.

This is my opinion. I understand that not everyone will see it this way, but I'd encourage you to truly consider this. I'm certainly not an expert. It's what God taught me through trial and error. Also, there are specific parameters in which I allowed tattling.

Kid one comes running to me. They start relaying "facts", something like...so and so did such and such. I do listen, but usually I would ask them, "Is your problem with me?" It wasn't. "Have you talked to so and so?" They hadn't. Maybe kid B comes running, "Kid A is doing such and such." My question to kid B, " Is there blood, fire or water?" Never did I get an affirmative answer. "Well, go talk to kid A"

Those are the most common ways I responded. It encouraged the kids to work together. It took me completely out of the equation. And, actually, it helped them think first and take their own emotion out of the situation.

If you ask my kids, they will tell you they learned to work out their differences, which helped them deal with other people as adults.

I call that a win. I am not that smart. God helped me see the bigger picture and He is the one who helped me see just how important sibling relationships are.

Mommy, you got this!!

Mommy Moment...

Another day of clearing tumbleweeds. Don't worry. I had supervision... five grandkids: ages 12, 10, 8, 6, and 4.

Our yard was filled with tumbleweeds! They don't usually pack in here like that, but they did, and they had to go. The 6-year-old and I went out early while the others were just sitting down to breakfast. We carefully started a fire in a clear area and began hauling tumbleweeds over one at a time. This kid is a "thinker". He likes facts and wants to know the how's and why's of what you're doing. I was careful to teach fire safety, as well as why these weeds were a danger around our house. He was great help! Once we had that area cleared, I sent him after the others. They worked with me for the next 2 hours! Again, I taught fire safety as we worked. They brought the weeds to within a few feet of the fire. I then could burn them one a time. They hauled them from all around our yard.

We were getting tired of it and they were beginning to slow down. I thought maybe I'd have to finish by myself. Not something I looked forward to because it would still take several more hours if I was to finish alone.

Out of the blue, the 12-year-old starts making it a game. "Hurry! We have to get this wall built! The enemy is coming! Look! They are tearing down the wall!" I became "the enemy." They were the wall builders.

That's all they needed to hear. Suddenly they were running to find more tumbleweeds and creating a "wall." I, the enemy, grabbed weeds and threw them into the fire.

I was so very grateful for that kid. He saw what was happening. He knew I wouldn't quit and that I would work alone, so he came up with a solution.

That's the kind of young men we want to raise! He took charge. Not in a rude demanding way. He made it a game and created an atmosphere of fun. What a great man he is!

I was sure to tell him that I saw great wisdom and leadership in him, that I was grateful and proud of him. He stood a little taller, a little straighter, after our talk.

Sweet Mommy, praise the good!! Call them up to leadership with kind reinforcement of what they do well. He may not remember playing games here with me, but he will never forget how proud I was of him. His heart will hold that feeling and look for ways to make me proud again. That's something you want in your children, your boys especially.

Mommy, you got this!!

Mommy Moment...

We've had a few fussy eaters in our home. I have babysat many, many children. It took me a while to figure out how to get a fussy eater to eat anything and everything I serve at mealtime. It has worked for family members, neighbor kids, kids I baby sat...bunches of kids.

First, I need to say, we eat meals together at the table. Kids aren't allowed to wander around with food, nor do they eat at separate times. We all gather at the table.

When we have a fussy eater in the house, I make sure to bake a batch of cookies, ones I know the fussy eater likes. Then I put one cookie for each person sharing mealtime with us onto a small plate. That plate is then placed in the center of the table during dinner. Mealtime proceeds as normal. I usually serve the food to any littles at our table, and I certainly do that for the fussy eater. I don't give them a full serving, just a small amount of each dish.

They may sit there and not eat or they may clear their plate. The choice is theirs completely. BUT...if they want the cookie that's right there in front of them, they must eat everything on their plate. It's their choice.

We all eat and then grab a cookie. If they haven't eaten their food, that leaves that 1 cookie sitting there, right in front of them, it calls to them.

Only once did I have a kid not clean up their meal. Kids who won't eat for their parents will eat every bit I give them...by their own choosing. No fuss. No fight.

Often, they discover they like the foods they wouldn't eat at home, and they ask for a second serving after they eat their cookie.

Sometimes a bit of incentive goes a long way!

Mommy, you got this!!

Mommy Moment...

I told you that my mother died the year before our 5th child was born. I didn't tell you the story.

Mom loved to dance. She and Dad took the kids, Curt and I with them square dancing until my dad was too ill to dance. Mom took line dancing lessons with Danielle when she was 70 and Danielle was 10. After Dad's death she continued to go dancing whenever she could. It was there that she got reacquainted with a man who had gone to school with her and grown up on an adjacent farm to hers. After a few months, he proposed. She was excited. Dad had died 3 years earlier, and although she was content, she was lonely.

I was a little concerned only because he had a grandson who was known to get into trouble, but Mom seemed so happy I didn't make a fuss. They married at the end of summer.

Curt's father died in an accident that November. Life was tough. We adored Curt's father, so we struggled in our grief. I didn't really notice that Mom had begun to pull away from us. She didn't let the kids stay with her as much. She didn't visit us like she used to. She didn't call as much. I didn't pause to think when she fell and broke a few ribs… twice.

One morning in spring Mom called. She was crying. She shared with me that she was being abused. She and I cried together. I begged her to come live with us. I told her we would figure out how to keep her safe and fix this mess. She made me promise not to tell my siblings just yet. She wanted a couple weeks to think. I later discovered from her neighbor that the police had been called to her home several times. I can't express my emotions at that time: confusion, fear, anger, guilt, heartbreak.

My birthday rolled around, and I realized she would never leave him. The reason I came to that thought is rather ridiculous. She gave me an orange mini skirt for my birthday. I don't care for orange. I have never worn a mini skirt. When I went to return it, I saw that those skirts were the display item closest to the door. She must have rushed in and bought the first thing she came to. That's when I knew… she was from a generation of women who believed that marriage was until death, she would stay with him until death separated them.

Memorial Day came just after that. She refused to go with me to visit the graves of her parents and my Dad. It was something we had done together my entire life…until then. I did go. I went all alone. I sat on my daddy's grave and sobbed. I cried so hard I felt like my chest would explode. Through my tears I begged God to help her. I pleaded with Him to get her out of that horrible situation. He did, but not in a way I would have ever expected, nor wanted.

She was killed in a car wreck one week later. They both died, actually.

I know it was an answer to my prayer. I know God took her home. I know she is safe with Him. But…I will never stop missing that amazing lady. Sweet Mommy, love your family with your whole heart. Make amazing memories with them.

Mommy, you got this!!

Mommy Moment…

Our fourth child has always been more verbal than most kids. Most babies coo and babble; this girl used words. By 10 months old she could speak in 3-word sentences!

It was quite a shock for people when they'd see us in the store and start to baby talk to her and she'd respond in a full sentence. The girl's ability to formulate her thoughts into words was, and is, amazing!

At a year old her favorite word was 'actually'. She knew how to use it even if she couldn't quite pronounce it. If someone accidentally called her the wrong name…"Aktshuly, I'm Kali."

If I said something incorrectly, "Aktshuly, mother…"

That's another thing, she called me mother, not mom or mommy, always 'mother'. I have no idea why. She just always did.

She was so determined to learn to read books like her older siblings that, even though she is dyslexic, she learned to read by age 4. The girl could read songs from a hymnal by then. She reads more books in one year than most of us do in 10.

There are times though when her brain gets ahead of her, and she says something all wrong. We call them "Kali-isms." Being the sweet family that we are we quote her odd sayings back to her as often as we can. A favorite is, "Out my mouth, left my brain."

Each child comes to the world as a baby. They may be tiny, but they are their own person. They aren't "mimi-me's." They are themselves. Our job as mommies is to help them see how precious and individual, they are. I have 5 kids. They are each different from the others. They each have different strengths and different needs. I encourage you, Sweet Mommy, to let them be themselves. Don't force them to be something you want them to be. Guide, encourage, love and train them, but let them be who God intends them to be. I struggled not to put my insecurities onto my kids. I also struggled not to hold them back. God helped me every step of the way. He will help you, too.

Mommy, you got this!!

Mommy Moment...

I must have been about twelve when I started doing my own laundry. I'm not sure how it started. We had moved from one small town to another, and my new room was in the basement, right by the laundry area, so it may have been simple logistics. I think that was only part of it.

Mom worked, as I have said, so she was busy. I did try to lighten her load by doing the dusting and such, so maybe that was part of it, too.

But I think I may have seen a commercial or TV show that talked about sorting laundry. I say that because I remember thinking I didn't want my whites to be pink. From then on, I did my own laundry. I can't imagine I did it well or kept up on it, but I was in charge of my own from then on.

My own kids started helping with laundry as soon as they could grab a wash rag and match the corners. They were tiny. Not that they were really any help, but they were right with me and doing the best they could. At 2 or so, they could fold towels and match socks. By 4 they could help sort and carry the clothes to the washer. We continued to work together even after they took over all their own laundry at 8.

Yes. Eight. Each one was put in charge of their own laundry then. I still helped a bit, but they were perfectly capable of doing it. The hard part for them was getting the clothes into the washer and then transferring the clean, wet ones into the dryer. Often, they had to push a chair up to the washer to be able to reach.

You might think I'm in the wrong for giving an 8-year-old that much responsibility. I might be, but It was good for them in so many ways. First, they learned how to do laundry well. Second, they didn't change clothes 47 times a day if they were the one washing it. Third, it helped them feel important and valuable. They contributed to the family. Boys especially need to feel grown up and capable.

Yes, there were times when they packed the washer too full, or forgot to pretreat a stain, but when is a better time to learn those types of lessons than when Mom is right here to help fix it.

Devin called from college one day. He explained to me that he had been teaching the other students, girls as well as boys, how to do laundry. Apparently, it wasn't a skill they had learned, so he had become the teacher of all things laundry. LOL

Sweet Mommy, find ways they can contribute to the family. It will lighten your load and it will help them feel good about who they are.

Mommy, you got this!!

Mommy Moment...

Our youngest was such a negotiator! It may have been because he was the youngest of 5, or maybe because the 2 siblings just older than him were sisters. I don't know why, but I do know it's true.

If he wanted a snack, but it was too close to mealtime, I would naturally tell him "no." He would then ask for an orange. "No." How about an apple?

In his little mind fruit wasn't a snack, so surely an orange would be ok. Well, if not an orange then an apple should be fine. At that point I'd ruffle his hair, give him a kiss and tell him to go play till mealtime.

Some days it was so exhausting to answer the same question so many times.

Here's the thing. He wasn't being naughty. He didn't mean to be disobedient. He just needed to clarify what I meant. His little brain needed me to be very clear.

Each kid has their own way of processing information. It takes true wisdom...and a huge amount of patience...to figure out how to relate to each child.

By the way, Caleb remembers negotiating with me. He also remembers me telling him he should grow up to be a used car salesman or a lawyer. -Careful what you tell your kids, they have the ability to remember every word.

Mommy, you got this!!

Mommy Moment...

Church should be a place of peace and comfort...but sometimes...when you have littles…

We were visiting a church that had a little balcony. It was an older building with beautiful woodwork. Normally we sit up front when we go to church, especially with our younger 3, but we decided to give in to the kids and we all sat in the balcony. They might have been 6, 8 and 10, possibly 8, 10 and 12, years old at this point. Surely, they were old enough to be quiet. It would be fun...so we thought.

This church served communion a bit differently than what we were used to. Everyone was asked to go forward, pick up the bread and juice, then return to their seats with them.

Nothing too complicated, just different. Curt and I spoke to the kids to make sure they understood what to do.

When the time came for those of us in the balcony to go down for communion, we quietly walked to the little wooden staircase...

It was narrow and had a couple turns with small landing areas. That meant 6 or 8 steps, a landing area 8 or 10 more and you are on the main floor.

...The church was somber and very quiet...until Caleb missed a step and Thunk, thunked down a couple stairs. Everyone gasped. He POPPED right up with a grin at the first landing and proceeded down. Most of the church tried NOT to laugh at his quick recovery, but there were a few muffled snickers. Down the next set of stairs, and...he slipped again. Thunk, thunk, THUD on the wooden stairs. He POPPED right up... with a great big smile!

There was no holding back the snickers this time... EVERYBODY laughed!

He recovered quickly, but I'm not so sure I did. Sweet Mommy, kids do things that draw attention. Don't panic, don't get embarrassed, and don't be angry, just roll with it and smile.

I bet no one remembers the sermon that day...but I have no doubt they remember the cute little guy that made them laugh.

Mommy, you got this!!

Mommy Moment...

Life was tough. I was struggling. There were a dozen things that played into the decision, but it was still a tough one to make. We put Devin into a small private middle school when he started 6th grade. I hated the decision, but I couldn't see any other answer. Danielle was already taking classes at the High School. Jenna was only 5, so her schooling was no issue.

Curt's father had died in November. Jenna needed dental work. My mom was killed in a car wreck in June. Her husband's daughter was making all sorts of demands. I had to be in the lawyer's office many,

many times. We were selling Mom's home. My emotions were a mess, and I hadn't the strength to homeschool Devin.

We had no extra money, so I agreed to become the lunch lady in exchange for his tuition. I'm not sure it was easier, but I didn't have to try to stay ahead of him academically. All I had to do was cook.

A neighboring family picked up Danielle and Devin each morning for school. The mom worked in town and was driving her own two in already. The kids were good friends, so it worked out well. At around 9 am, I would call the school and get the lunch count. Next, the little girls and I would go grocery shopping for lunch. We cooked at a local church and hauled lunch over to the school. After cleanup, the girls and I would head to our own church and they would lie down and nap till 3. Many days I napped along with them. Once we were awake, we were to pick up our older two and the neighbor two and take everyone home.

I felt like a failure. I felt like I had abandoned the call that God had given me. I felt sad for the time I would not have with the older two. I felt I was cheating the younger two out of the simple life of being at home. I was depressed.

I knew we were doing all we could. I knew I was not the best teacher for Devin in my state of emotional turmoil. Yet, it broke my heart. So many days while the girls were napping, I would lie there and cry until I cried myself to sleep.

This is the situation we were in when I got pregnant with Caleb. This and many other emotional fights were taking place in my heart.

Sweet Mommy, you may go through tough stuff. You may have to make tough decisions. Some may break your heart, but I promise, if you can hold on and look for the good and lean on God, it will get better. I do wish there had been a way we could have homeschooled that year. I do wish I could have found the strength to be teacher for my 12-year-old, as well as the others, but I know God understood. He knew my heart.

He knew my hurt. He never let me go, even when I could barely hold on to Him.

Mommy, you got this!!

Mommy Moment...

I came home from the store yesterday to find as I opened the door from the garage to the house that "someone" had FILLED the entry area with balloons! Large ones and small ones, but all brightly colored poured through the doorway as I came into the house.

The next thing I saw was crepe paper streamers zigzagging across the entire dining, living and kitchen areas of the house. They went from light fixture to light fixture, and from cupboard to picture, all across the house.

I found the table covered in flowers and gifts (including a piñata). Then I noticed a sweet friend hiding just out of sight.

That was yesterday. Today our eldest daughter and her family came with homemade ice-cream, gifts of all sorts and another pinata. She has seven littles. Each one came in with a gift for me. Each gift a thoughtful expression of their love. -- The 6-year-old has worked for days to make dandelion jelly just for me.

Everyone was talking and laughing so loudly that I could hardly hear Jenna on our Zoom call.

You see my sweet family along with a few sweet young friends chose to surprise me with a bit of a party. Yes. They blindfolded me, spun me around, and handed me a bat to break open those pinatas. It was a bit ridiculous.

We had a lovely day.

I absolutely loved the time with them all. It was fun for me to watch them all visit and interact with each other. They are quite special to me.

I know I shouldn't, but I couldn't help but cry. I am nothing special. I have done nothing but live a simple life as a wife and mother. I haven't changed the world, solved world hunger or done anything that society would see as valuable. Yet today these precious people made me feel so loved, so valued. My heart is overwhelmed.

On the days when motherhood is a struggle, take heart, Sweet Mommy, the difficult days will pass. There will come a day when your sweet littles will stand with you as adults and you will see that the difficult days were all worth it. Those days where you feel like you are a mean mom, a weary mom, a frustrated mom, are all a part of your journey, but they aren't the end.

The Bible has a verse in it that says something like…Her children rise up and call her blessed; her husband also, and he praises her. My prayer for you, Sweet Mommy, is that your children will do just that, and that you will see just how important motherhood is to the next generation.

Mommy, you got this!!

Mommy Moment...

The day our chicks came was always a highlight of the year.

Baby chicks are so cute! We would order 75 to 100 of them each year. Twenty-four were egg laying breeds. The rest were raised for meat.

We would move a small horse trough into the kitchen, put an inch or so of pine shavings to cover the bottom, we add a waterer, a tray of food and suspend a heat lamp in the tank.

Yes. I did say we would move it into the kitchen. Baby chicks can't regulate their temperature, they need to be closely watched. It was easier to have them here in the house.

It's quite entertaining to put a blade of grass or a fresh picked weed in with them. It's a bit like watching a tiny soccer game. One chick picks up the grass and runs around the tank. Chick 2 snatches it from number 1 and HE runs off with the grass. Then a third snatches it and the game continues! We all loved picking some greenery and starting the game. It's hilarious to watch!

The kids loved holding them. The problem with that is…holding baby chicks too much often kills them. They are fragile little creatures. Although, they did kill a few with kindness, the kids were never mean.

Chicks have no way of taking care of themselves. They need care. Kids are like that. They may have opinions and make demands, but they don't have the wisdom to see beyond the immediate irritation to know what's best. They need Parents to teach and train them. They need mommies to make decisions for them. Some of those decisions are not easy. Sweet Mommy, much of their care is up to you. I know it gets to be a heavy load. Take heart. God will give you all the wisdom you need if you will just ask.

Mommy, you got this!!

Mommy Moment...

I've gardened since Curt and I were first married. I'm still challenged by it!

At first it was amazing! Curt's Dad told me what to do, I did it, and we had a great garden. Then it was just me and my kids. THAT was totally different. I am not as good at instructing as he was. Some of our seeds were too deep, some too shallow, some too close together and others way too far apart. But you know what? It didn't matter. God took care of the plants and we had plenty to harvest.

I think we were short on carrots 3 years in a row. One year they didn't come up. They were planted too deep. Another year, one sweet child washed them out with the water. I believe they got sprayed with weed killer the third year.

One year we had a terrible storm come through the first week in June. The garden was destroyed by hail. It was heartbreaking. The garden had been so pretty. The kids and I replanted everything. Our growing season is long enough that we thought we would still be able to harvest plenty. Nope. Two other hailstorms came through that year. One the first week of July and the next one the first week of August! We replanted some things in July, but when it was hailed the third time, I told God He would have to provide for us some other way. He did. I had a friend who had far too much in her garden that year. We ended up with more than enough produce.

Maybe I should explain the size of our garden. It usually has 50 rows. Each row is 50 feet long. We plant a full row of green beans, three of peas, and 16 to 20 of corn. We have 30 or more tomato plants. I think you get the idea. It's not a small undertaking. I garden because I like having fresh produce for my family. I like knowing how our food was grown and what chemicals, if any, were applied to it. I don't even enjoy the planting and weeding. Well, that's only half true. I enjoy working with my kids. I don't enjoy the work itself. Now that I don't have them with me it's just work. No fun at all.

The kids are grown, and we don't need so much produce any more, but I struggle not to plant all 50 rows. This year we are attempting to downsize the garden. I planted all the same things just much smaller quantities. For instance, I only have 10 tomatoes not 30. I will keep you updated on how it turns out.

Growing a garden is much like growing children. Both need careful and intentional care. Expert or mentor advice is oh so helpful. And you will do a whole lot of watering, weeding and tending before you ever see any harvest. Storms may come. It may seem like the work never ends. But…when God sends the harvest it is an amazing time!!!

Mommy, you got this!!!!

Mommy Moment...

I have told you the story of Caleb's birth and my pregnancy issues, but I left out why we chose his name. We feel quite strongly about the meaning of names, and the significance of each name chosen.

Curt and I wanted to honor our family's grandfathers. We considered Isaiah, Jens, Gerald, and even Delmore. In the last few weeks of the pregnancy, we had settled on Isaiah. It was not only Curt's grandfather's name, but we liked that it was a Biblical name. From then until his birth, I spoke of our baby as Isaiah.

-My sister called him "Baby Buddha", but that was because of my shape those last couple of months.

You know he came quite quickly, that's true. Once the cord stopped pulsing and Curt cut it, we laid our sweet baby boy on the bed just to look at him and thank God for him. As we watched him, we realized he wasn't all curled up like most newborns. He laid there with his legs out straight and his arms stretched out on the bed. He wasn't crying. He was looking around wide eyed and content. Curt and I were astonished.

Simultaneously we both thought of the story in the Bible of Caleb. He had been sent to a new land and when others were afraid of the people there, Caleb saw the amazing provisions and said the new land was good.

Our little baby was in a "new land" and he looked so happy and content. We couldn't help but name him Caleb.

In His Word, God tells several stories of changing people's names. He tells of Angels speaking to people and telling mothers what the name of the child should be. I feel like He named Caleb, not us. And the name definitely suits him. The kid is in his twenties and still has that happy-go-lucky attitude and is perfectly content wherever he is.

Sweet mommy, God knows your name, and it's important to Him. He adores you. Seek Him. He is waiting for you to look to Him.

Mommy, you got this!!

Mommy Moment...

The girls and I had a little dress shop that we loved to go to. The owner was a kick! She had such fun clothes: jeans, tops, dresses even formal gowns! Bonus. She carried tall and skinny items. The girls were so skinny in high school and so tall, it was difficult to find clothes that fit and were cute.

I have no idea why I went in that day. I'm sure I was looking for jeans or something for the girls.

The owner had just received a shipment of formal gowns. They were stunning! Not your typical prom gowns, more what you'd see at a formal gala event. There was this one...silver, sequins, V-neck, mermaid...WOW! She thought I should try it on.

Wait right there. I could no more afford that dress than a new Lamborghini. She didn't care.

She brought the dress to me and told me to put it on.

I laughed! The size was too small.

"No." she said. 'It needs to FIT tight."

Just so you all know I am tall, 5'10+ and I am skinny. But...my height makes me look littler than I am. I haven't worn a '0' since high school.

She was determined that the dress she handed me would fit, so I trusted that she knew the sizing.

Well. It fit! She was all proud of HOW it fit. I felt a bit like I was a marshmallow being shoved into a piggybank!

That's not the worst of it. I couldn't get out of it!

I'm so serious. I was stuck in an expensive dress in the dressing room of the shop.

She didn't believe me for a bit. Then she tried to help. Then we got to laughing...

It was so mortifying and hilarious at the same time. I didn't have to go home in a $600 gown. She did get me out of it without damaging the gown.

Next time you go to try on clothes I hope you think of me and smile.

Mommy, you got this!!

Mommy Moment...

When Danielle and Jeff first married, Jeff was in the Navy. That meant they had to live near an ocean. There are none in Colorado, so we traveled quite a bit for about 7 years. First to South Carolina and then to Washington state near Seattle.

Having our eldest child that far from home was a strange thing for us. When Jeff was deployed, we didn't want her alone so we traveled to her as often as we could. She also came home at times, but she had tiny babies whereas I had older kids.

I can tell you, traveling to Washington from Colorado in the winter is NOT the best idea! One year we left home in a blizzard. We literally took back roads from our house to get around a closed highway. All the way along the states were closing the roads just after we drove them. By the time we were out of Colorado, Wyoming and Utah Curt was exhausted! We stopped for a bit of sleep in Idaho and continued in the morning. Again, the roads were miserable!

It wasn't just Christmas that we were concerned with. We probably would have just waited a day or two if that was the only reason we were going. Danielle was expecting their third child that year. The Navy had changed some of Jeff's schedule and we weren't sure if he would be home or out on a submarine. We felt like we absolutely had to keep going and get to Danielle as soon as we could, so that she would have help with her older two kids when the baby came.

We were somewhere in Washington when Jeff called. He let us know that he was home with the kids and Danielle was at the hospital with their new son. We were thrilled to hear his voice and know that she was not alone.

Don't feel bad for us. God watched over us the entire way. Yes. It was unwise to keep going in such bad weather conditions. If Curt had not been driving, I never would have attempted the trip. He felt confident that we were fine. God was with us and would get us safely to Danielle.

Mommies worry about their kids no matter how old they are. That year Danielle had three of her own, but I was still so concerned for her welfare that we drove for 2 days in blizzard conditions. A mommy's heart always feels responsible for her babies…even if those babies have babies of their own.

Mommy, you got this!!

Mommy Moment...

I don't know what your family does when it's time for baby to go to sleep, here were rocked our babies, naptime or bedtime, it didn't matter. We loved to rock them.

I absolutely loved the quiet moments sitting in the rocking chair singing quietly as I stared at the sweet little babe in my arms…or wrestled the orangutan I called my child…whichever was true at that moment. Looking at their faces, holding then gently as I patted their back or stroked their arm brought such peace and joy to my heart. Even now if I get the chance to rock a baby it thrills my heart!

Our littles, all five, had to be able to go to sleep wherever we were. For the older two that meant at either Grandma's, maybe in the car or a tractor, possibly at one aunt's or another and definitely at church. For the younger three it meant all those places plus all the sports events, 4-H meetings, competitions, and activities of the older two. I NEEDED my babies to be able to sleep ANYWHERE.

By the time we had Caleb I carried a sleeping bag in the car wherever we went so that I could lay him down once he went to sleep. That kid slept on that sleeping bag at tennis matches, shooting matches, and soccer games all around our county.

I have since learned that if a child has a "trigger" some something that happens every time they go to sleep, they soon respond to that "trigger" no matter where they are. I didn't know that as a new mom. I didn't know that until my kids were passed the baby stage. What I did know was that if I gently rubbed their arm, sang the same nursery songs and rocked, either in a rocking chair or just swaying back and forth, my babies went right to sleep.

The totally awesome part is that I got several extra minutes every day with my babies, peaceful, sometimes prayerful, moments. I so needed those moments. Life was extremely difficult at times. Sitting still and watching them sleep was therapeutic. It reminded me just why I loved being mommy. It helped me refocus my thoughts and eliminate the feelings of worthlessness that I battled.

That tiny baby in my arms needed me and loved me. God trusted ME with that little life.

Maybe the rocking was as much for me as it was for them.

Mommy, you got this!!

Mommy Moment...

You know we live on a farm. Farm life is a great deal of work, but I wouldn't trade it for the world!!

We always had a small herd of sheep, thirty or so ewe lambs (momma sheep) and a buck (daddy sheep). They were a necessary evil. Necessary, because they are awesome at eating weeds and keeping an area from becoming overtaken by weeds. It's nice to have them eat the grass out under our trees in our windbreak areas. Evil, well, that might not be quite the right term, but they can be quite a headache.

They jump fences. They eat the wrong things. They have to be sheared, because they don't shed, and they will overheat in the summer. I think they are born trying to die. I mean it. As cute and sweet as they are, they seem to want to do all the things that will get them killed. You really have to watch them closely. They will get their heads stuck in things. They will try to jump over things and plow headfirst into them instead. And, you may not know it, but they will, especially when they are young, eat so much that they will kill themselves. It's strange.

Jenna had one old lamb that we could put on a halter. She was very tame. One day she had a wild thought and started to run. Curt got a hold on the rope, but she didn't stop. It was a bit of a rodeo. He had quite a struggle getting her settled down. Before it was all over the rope had burned off the skin on 2 of his fingers clear down to the bone. It was terrible. A nurse friend told us how to deal with the wound and although it took a while his hand healed completely and didn't scar.

We tenderly and intentionally cared for each lamb. We hoped and prayed each momma would have twins. Not only does that increase the herd, but it means the babies are a bit smaller and easier for the mommies to deliver. We watched their feed. We kept their water fresh. We added bedding to their pens. We were good to them, even put their welfare before our own. We loved them.

I've often wondered why God chooses to call us sheep. Are we really like that? Are we born trying to die? Although I do see some obvious parallels, I'm not sure I understand why He does it.

Maybe it's not just that we are like sheep. Maybe it's the fact that God is the Good Shepherd. He tenderly and intentionally cares for each of us. He wants the best for us. He watches over us. Maybe He calls us His sheep, not because of who WE are but because of who HE is.

Mommy, you got this!!

Mommy Moment...

When the kids were little, I quickly learned that I couldn't give them choices if there was only one acceptable answer. Let me try to make that make sense.

At first, I would ask Danielle things like," Do you want to go to the store with me?" It's a simple question, but there is only one acceptable answer, "Yes" If she were to say no, then what? Would I not go grocery shopping because a 2-year-old said no? Instead I learned to say, "Do you want to go shopping now or after your nap?" After a few years of motherhood, I learned it was even better to happily call out, "Get your shoes. We are going shopping." No question asked. I would use a happy sing song voice and make it sound super fun, and I did make it fun. They were quick to comply.

When it came to clothing I might give them a choice of 2 appropriate outfits, but they didn't really choose their own clothes until they were old enough to know that dirty chore clothes were not the right choice for going into the store or church.

Meals were much the same, and here is why. Although I already had kind of gotten the hang of mothering, I learned of a sweet mommy with 4 kids who was known to make a separate meal for each kid every single day! That poor woman!! She was frazzled to the core. Nothing she cooked made them all happy on any given day. Child A might have eaten Mac and Cheese just last week, but if she made it in hopes of pleasing Child A and Child B, Child A suddenly hated it and refused to eat it. At that point the poor dear would make something else for Child A, and she was probably making totally different food for C and D already because they refused it to begin with. Mealtime took hours and was horribly distressing.

Sweet Mommy, you will save yourself so much heartache and stress if you don't get into this habit. It's ok to NOT have their approval for everything you do. It sounds so harsh as I reread that. I don't mean to be harsh, not at all. My hope is to save you from the heartache. You, Sweetheart, have been given the role of MOTHER. God made you the "CEO" of your household. It's ok to behave like one.

And another problem, when I did forget and asked a question that they answered in a way I was not happy with, I had only one real option. I could ignore what they choose and do my own thing. In doing so I inadvertently taught them two terrible things: 1, their opinion doesn't matter, and 2, I lie, because I told them they could choose, but didn't let them.

I wanted my kids to trust me. I needed them to trust me. To do that I must always be a trustworthy person, even in the seemingly little things.

Mommy, you got this!!

Mommy Moment...

We have a small flock of hens. When all the kids were home, we had 25 to 30 hens. The kids tended them and gathered the eggs. I kept all the eggs that we needed as a family, but the rest were theirs to sell for spending money.

Now, it's not necessary to have that many. I keep 8 hens and have eggs aplenty most of the time. I had the extras so we could sell the eggs. The kids were allowed to keep all egg proceeds as long as they tended the chickens.

When Jenna was little, she made pets out of several hens. She taught one to sit on her shoulder. Henny was a dear little hen. She liked to be where Jenna was. She would follow Jenna around. She was a plump little black and white Plymouth Rock. I usually raise Leghorns simply because they lay an egg nearly every day, but we often let the kids choose a different breed of chick as their special chicken. Anyway... Henny was a favorite. She kept an eye out for Jenna and would come right over to the gate for her.

Hens each have a definite attitude. Some are super compliant. Others are super sassy. Some like to complain and cluck continually when you are in their pen. We have had a couple that so liked their eggs that they would peck you if you tried to take eggs out from under them. I always wondered if those ones would have enough sense to hatch their eggs. I refuse to keep a rooster, so I never did find out.

Children are like that, each one very individual. They can be compliant, sassy, curious, and funny. Some have an extraordinary number of words to use every day. Others are happy to quietly do their own thing. The hard part is figuring out the personality of each one and teaching them obedience without damaging their God given personality. It takes true wisdom, patience and love. Sweet mommy, you can do it! You are amazing! You love your kids, and they want to please you. Just as Jenna spent time learning how to train her little hen and I learned the "language" of my kids. You will have to spend time learning what makes each child tick. You will learn what thrills their heart and what breaks it. You will find there is tremendous joy in simply "being" with your own little chicks.

Mommy, you got this!!

Mommy Moment...

My daughter Danielle says that babies have never been inconvenienced. That's why they cry about everything that doesn't go their way. We have to teach and train them what things are worth crying over. I am oh so much the same way. I don't like to be inconvenienced.

When I pray for something specific, I often forget that God doesn't have to answer immediately. He might, but He might be waiting until I have the correct attitude, or maybe the timing isn't right. I do know that He wants my best, but…all too often I want what I want, and I want it right now!

We have one of those scenarios currently going on in our world. For three years now our son in law has planned to retrain from one area to another in the Air Force. He had everything set and had just a few weeks to wait to leave for Special Forces training when he tore his Achilles tendon. That made him ineligible for his retraining. So, he waited and healed, and made a new plan. Again, his plans were thwarted. They were transferred to another base. He made a new plan, language school. Everything was in order…or so he thought. After doing all the right things and getting all but the final approval, he was told he had to be at the new base 2 full years before he would be eligible to retrain and start language school. It was quite a blow!

Can you relate? Have you had times like that? Times when you just had to stop and say, "God I have no idea what you are doing or what you want me to do…but I love you. I trust that you have a plan. I will wait on you. And, Lord, I will love and serve you no matter what." A scene from the movie "Facing the Giants" comes to mind.

I spoke with Him and with our daughter. We concluded that it was time to 'be still' and learn to be content right where they were, and they did. That was a month ago.

Here's the cool part…

God opened a slot in that very language school. Our son in law was the only candidate who met all the requirements. HE GOT THE SLOT!! He has two weeks to plan and get moved! God is amazing!!

We could not be prouder of the kid if he was our own child!! We have all been praying for this for quite a while. God sees a bigger picture, and I know He has an amazing plan!

If God had answered "yes" when we were first praying about a retrain, we would not have had the extra years with them at the base near us. We would not have had them here for holidays and birthdays for the extra years. They would not have been nearby when they had their first child. I would not have been able to be at the birth of that child. I can see so many reasons why God waited for this answer. I am repentant for my impatience and humbled by His grace and mercy.

I'm sure I will be impatient again and want what I want, but I hope I will remember to trust that God wants my best and I can just 'be still.'

Mommy, you got this!!

Mommy Moment...

Just before Jenna had that terrible motorcycle accident, she had been chosen to play the piano at a State conference for Homeschool families. It's quite an honor to be chosen. It is a huge conference. She had also earned the right to go to a national shooting sports competition with her air-rifle by placing top at the state level that same year. Another amazing accomplishment.

The girl had worked for several months to learn and then memorize a 7-minute-long classical piece by Debussy. If you don't play let me just tell you a 7-minute piece is incredibly long! Learning the song was difficult enough, but to memorize it was amazing. She had also been meeting with the other members of the shooting team to practice together.

Then came her accident. If you remember, she wasn't badly hurt, no broken bones, no internal injuries. But…she had "road rash" and bruising all up and down her left side and had stretched a tendon in her left hand. The "road rash" and bruising healed quite quickly. The tendon not so much. She wore a brace for several weeks.

That's where the problem was, she couldn't practice for either event with that brace on.

That didn't stop our determined little 16-year-old, no way! She still practiced playing our piano every day for 45 minutes to an hour. She made every shooting sports practice as well.

When the day of the State Homeschool Conference came she was ready and played beautifully! I was amazed and overwhelmed with pride and joy listening to her play for them, because I had watched her struggle to practice.

As for her air-rifle competition, she did well there, too. It's a 3-day event. The kids practice and then shoot each day. Each competitive round takes about 45 minutes. The kids get into position and then hardly move until they have completed all their shots. Our girl would remove her brace, complete the round and put her brace back on. Her hand ached each and every day. It wasn't easy, but she did her very best and scored quite well in spite of her injury.

I've learned a lot from that girl. She had committed to something and she wasn't going to let anything stop her from her commitments. She struggled! And yet, she persevered.

For me, parenting was a bit like that. It was a struggle. I loved my kids, but I didn't really know what I was doing. I had to practice even when it was hard, even when it brought me to tears because it hurt. In the end, the rewards of having 5 amazing adult children was worth it, but it was no easy feat. Watching Jenna struggle through to complete the tasks before her reminded me that just because something is difficult it doesn't mean you can quit or even should quit. Usually, it the tough stuff in my life that taught me the most. The things I had to fight for are the ones that brought the greatest rewards.

Mommy, you got this!!

Mommy Moment...

Ever feel like you're the worst mommy in the world? I did fairly often. Even now I do occasionally.

Jenna was 2. She was such a little doll! We were having dinner, and she was in her highchair.

Our highchair was an antique wooden one with an adorable decal of a bear on the chair seat back. It had been Curt's as a baby. Oh, so many littles had used that chair!

Well, Jenna had gotten into the habit of pressing her feet against the table. At times she pressed hard enough to lift the front two legs off the floor and tip the chair back a bit. This day she must have been feeling extra strong...or extra naughty. She pressed hard against the table and the entire seat disconnected from its legs. She landed flat on her back on the floor... still in her seat!

Shocked and horrified I leaned down to comfort my wailing child and see what injuries she had. She was fine...just shaken a bit.

I felt terrible. I knew the legs were a little loose. I should have glued them.

Curt reminded me that she had been asked many times not to put her feet on the table. He also reminded me that we had warned her that the chair might tip over. She understood what we said even if she didn't fully comprehend the consequences.

I still felt bad.

Here's the deal, Sweet Mommy, she disobeyed. She chose to push on the table with her feet. Now, I would so much rather she had listened and obeyed, but she didn't. Her consequence must be hers. I should not carry guilt over her choice. For me, it is difficult not to feel bad when a child makes a poor choice. I want to fix it or stop it from happening, but that isn't in their best interest. They must learn to want to be nice and obey.

I still cried, but I knew she had to make mistakes and learn things for herself.

Mommy, you got this!!

Mommy Moment...

Do you know that you are doing one of the most difficult jobs on earth? You are attempting to raise good, honest, helpful, moral, God fearing, loving little human beings. I don't know about you, but I had no training. I didn't even have any experience to speak of. I didn't know how to cook or clean or budget or meet the hundreds of needs that a child has every day. Some of you are like that too. Others have some knowledge, maybe from experience or from college.

Here's the deal. All mommies have moments when they feel overwhelmed or unprepared. It's what you do in those moments that matters.

God entrusted you. He knows you've got this. Just pray. He will answer. Whether you are a dear friend of His or just an acquaintance, He still loves you.

I have heard from many that they struggle with depression of one sort or another. It happens to the best of mommies. It doesn't mean you don't love your kids. It means you hurt. For some of you it will pass quickly, for others it becomes an emotional pit that you can't quite get out of.

Please, Sweet Mommy, if you are depressed or sad find someone to talk to, someone who will listen and not try to fix you. If prayer is your thing, pray. If not, confide in someone who loves you. Even writing you thoughts and feelings down may help.

When I struggled, I didn't tell a soul. I don't want that for you. I may not know you personally, but I still care about you. May God bring His peace, His love, and return His joy to your heart.

Mommy, you got this!!

Mommy Moment...

Once Devin came along, I began to change my parenting… unfortunately. With Danielle I had been very consistent and on top of bad behavior yet encouraging to her heart. Then, I began to listen to the world. Society said children should be free to make choices. They should be free to express their emotions. Parents should respect those choices and emotions. Parents should not spank, but instead, use time-out, or talk with the child to explain your displeasure. Even well-meaning Christian leaders were saying not to discipline the child until they were nearly 2 years of age, because young children don't understand. So…I backed down. By the time my happy, joyful little guy was 5 or 6 I had confused him greatly. At 9 and 10 we struggled.

You see, he was super sharp and has a strong personality. When I no longer punished lying, he lied more. When I acted like playing rough was ok, he played rougher. When he was sassy and disrespectful, yet I did nothing, I encouraged the behavior. That's on me. I knew in my heart that God wanted me to parent. His word says clearly what is expected from a parent, yet I became timid and at times let behaviors slide. I could see that he just needed to know that I loved him and cared enough to be just and truthful. He knew full well what behavior was acceptable. Yet, my parenting was inconsistent and full of emotion. I felt as lost as he felt.

I have said that he had a strong will, he did, but that was not the core of the bad behavior. He has a heart for justice. He couldn't understand why I allowed him to sass me or act with disrespect and disobedience. Life got rough as I began to see my tragic mistake. I returned to being the "mean mom" (as my sister called me) and then he pushed against the rules even harder for a bit.

All of that could have been avoided. If I had held firm and parented with dignity and grace, we would not have had to fight so hard. If I had set rules and consequences and not given in to what others thought, he would not have had to misbehave to get my attention. He needed me to be firm yet loving and consistent.

Yes. He has a strong personality. All of our kids do. I want them to be strong in their convictions and strong in their faith. I want them to be able to stand against the tide of sinfulness that is prevalent in our society. I want them to have a strong character. There is nothing wrong with that. But how much time I wasted. How much emotional turmoil I created all because I wouldn't follow what God said. How sad.

There are those kids who test the rules and are strong willed, but, as in my case, the emotional turmoil wasn't the child's fault. It was my fault for listening to the world around me and trying to use the world's wisdom. I pray that you can learn from my mistake.

Mommy, you got this!!

Mommy Moment...

It is a difficult task to choose which of the kids have the strongest will. At first glance people might say that Devin has the strongest will, but all of them will "plant their feet" and not change their minds. The trick as Mommy was to outsmart their attitude.

"You have to clean your room today."

"NO."

"Oh, so you don't want to walk down to Dad." I would choose the one thing I knew they couldn't resist, for our kids, time with Dad was a HUGE treat. I could have used other things: no Ice cream, no friends coming over, no phone, cleaning the bathroom also, etc. But…you MUST be willing to follow through! You cannot say something that you aren't willing to do. Ours made the wrong choice a few times. That's ok, I didn't mind. They had to know that I meant every word I said. That is the key. They must believe you.

Here is another example…

"NO. I don't like that," is a statement that most mothers have heard, especially at the dinner table. Several of my kids said it, too. With our older kids I would respond, "You WILL eat that. Like it or not." With our younger ones I changed my tactics. I would instead reply matter-of-factly, "OK. Then you won't get a cookie." And I would walk away from the table, removing the cookies if they were on the table.

Do you see the difference? At first, I was choosing to argue with them. In the second example, I was gently giving them a negative consequence if they made the choice to not eat what was before them. I can't think of a time when they didn't eat what was before them if I simply made doing what I asked a much more appealing choice. Every picky eater that I have ever babysat made the right choice, too.

In the case of meals, if they didn't eat a meal, I truly did set it in the fridge at the end of dinner time and they were given that very same plate of food for as many meals as necessary to eat it all. I learned that after choosing to battle over meals with Devin. I am not proud of the fact that I could not outthink him when it came to meals. Kali was the pickiest about foods. She soon learned that I truly meant it when I said, "You will get nothing else until its gone." When the other kids were having a snack, I would set the plate of uneaten dinner in front of her. At the next meal, it sat in her place again. It's not so fun to push Mommy if Mommy doesn't get riled up. In our home we ate 3 meals and had a morning and an afternoon snack. It only took a couple of times for her to figure it out.

She is the one who learned to say, "You don't have to like it. You just have to eat it."

She was staying with a friend once and the mother asked her what she thought of dinner. To my horror, instead of being polite and saying something nice about the meal, the girl replied, "You don't have to like it. You just have to eat it." That poor mommy wasn't sure what to say to THAT.

It's important to start when they are little. It can be done with older kids, but it is much more painful for everyone involved. If you are struggling, come up with a strategy that you can truly follow through with. It isn't easy. I don't mean to make it sound that way. Motherhood is not for the faint of heart. You got to be strong, Sweet Mommy.

Mommy, you got this!!

Mommy Moment...

Our kids were a happy bunch. Our days were simple and scheduled. The rules were clear. And the kids were free to be themselves. That does not mean everything was perfect. We had messy days, just like every family. But I discovered after a few years that I am the thermostat not the thermometer in our family. I set the emotional temperature. That just means I learned how to set the tone in our home.

What does that mean? A thermostat sets the temperature in your home, cold or hot, it's determined by the thermostat. It was not an easy lesson, and its one I have to relearn every now and again. If my heart is settled and peaceful, our house is too. If I speak with tenderness, they do. If I am rattled and frustrated, the same will be true of our household. And, If I am angry and rude, well, that's the atmosphere of our home.

If I was stressed, that would be the day that one of the kids, or maybe all of them, would push the rules all day. I remember thinking, "Can't you just be good?" "Can't you just listen?"

Here's the thing, they couldn't. My own unsettled heart would cause me to be short tempered and harsh. Therefore, they would react to those sharp words with sassy answers and bad attitudes. Can you see how this could escalate? It did some days, I'm sad to say. My attitude hurt their hearts, so their behavior would be naughty.

Try this with your kids. Whisper all day. Don't explain anything or warn them, just start the day by whispering. See how they respond. I tried it. Truly. If I spoke in whispers it wasn't long and they would be whispering too. It's the same with a happy attitude. If I had one, they soon did too.

Have you ever tried jumping on their bed and singing "Rise and shine and give God the glory, glory." It's a short be happy song to start their day. I have done it many times...still do occasionally. They might grumble at first, but they would soon be singing that song, too, and it would get stuck in their heads and they would sing it all day.

There are many ways to change the atmosphere in your home. The whispering, the singing of silly songs, or maybe just doing your own favorite silly thing can reset your heart and theirs. And, really that is the issue...your heart. Find a way to be joyful yourself and it will change the atmosphere of your home. It isn't easy. Many days, I would stop and pray. I would ask God to help me. He always did. He will help you, too, if you ask.

Mommy, you got this!!

Mommy Moment...

Strong wills and determined attitudes can make a mommy more than a little frustrated. Every one of our kids had days or seasons when they had one or both.

If you have a child, you will have days when they are determined not to do as you have asked them to do. That's just normal. They are little people trying to be big. Some, like Danielle, are more compliant in general. Others, like our Miss Kali, are more determined. But both of those girls are easy to get along with, sweet ladies. And, both of them have a strength of character that won't bend. I use these two as examples because as adults, they are very similar, but as children, they were quite different.

Danielle was a rule follower. Kali made the rules. Danielle would do anything I asked. Kali needed a reason to do what I asked and needed time to think about it. It would have been easy to compare the two and be frustrated with Kali. Instead, I honored them both and we got along well…still do.

It would have been easy to push Danielle, to control her. She was compliant and I was Mommy. I had to learn to honor her heart and NOT ask too much of her. God made her just the way He wanted her. I had to be sure to let her be that easy-going girl. I had to let her mature at her own pace.

Kali, on the other hand, has a strong personality and therefore strong opinions. As a little one she would get frustrated and possibly rude if I told her directly what to do. She was in no way disobedient, she just needed me to speak in a different tone and word things in a way that her heart could hear me.

Let me try to give you an example.

I could tell Danielle, "Go get your shoes on." She would happily go do as asked. But if I wanted that same happy response from Kali, I had to reword it. "We are going to town. You will need to get your shoes." She would happily comply.

If we were going somewhere different, maybe to go visit someone that the kids didn't know or maybe even just grocery shopping on a different day. I could tell Danielle what we were going to do just before we needed to leave. Not so with Kali. I learned to tell her what was happening as soon as the decision was made. That way she could process the change of schedule and prepare her heart for the change. Then, when it was time to leave, she was happy as a lark and very obedient.

Each child is different. God made them just the way he wanted them. Their wills can be taught to obey in a pleasant way. It takes wisdom to speak to their hearts. Our challenge is to find a way to speak to the heart of the child so that they are not frustrated.

I expected all 5 of our kids to be obedient, kind and respectful. My expectations were the same, but I came to understand that each child was different and had to be treated as individuals.

Mommy, you got this!!

Mommy Moment...

One last thought on strong wills…

I love my strong-willed kids… all 5 of them. We didn't hit the "terrible two's" as some folks call it. Yes, they had days that they weren't as agreeable as others, but it wasn't a daily fight. I actually quite enjoyed them all at that age. It's when their personality really comes to light. The first two years are mostly about basic needs, but at about a eighteen months things change. I enjoyed figuring out how to reach their hearts.

At two everything is new and exciting. They are learning verbal communication. All the words they have listened to, they now are trying to say. They are becoming a little independent. No longer does Mommy have to do everything for them. They can, for instance, put their shoes on and use a spoon to feed themselves. They suddenly have opinions that they want to express. They may have a favorite pair of pants. They can't tell Mommy that they like the way they feel, but they always want that one pair. They can be a helper. They have watched their parents put dishes in the dishwasher, so they put everything in there, a teddy bear or blocks may go in. They are a watcher of people, they study them. Their emotions are quite evident to everyone around them. They don't have the vocabulary to express WHY they are frustrated, so they holler and stomp their foot. They see the sadness in someone's expression, but they don't understand it. It makes them feel on edge to see Mommy cry, and when they are on edge, they do naughty things. Not because they want to be naughty, but because they are responding to the emotional turmoil in others. At two, they know which adult will let them do as you please, they understand who is in charge. If the adults around them aren't confident in their parenting, they know it and will try to fill that top spot.

All of those things make being a two-year-old fun, but also make it challenging to be a parent. If you have been able to teach your families rules to your child before their second birthday, you will breeze right through them being two. If you have not, you may have a bit of a struggle.

I have said many times, look for the heart of the behavior. By that I mean, don't be pulled into the emotion on display, but sort out what it is rooted in. A lack of sleep is a common root of bad behavior. They need more sleep than we often realize. A need for undivided attention is another. If you can get ahold of a copy of the book "Love Languages" and study it, you may find that your child has a different love language than you do. Knowing what makes them FEEL loved may help bring peace into your home. I know you love them with all your heart, but their heart may not be hearing that in a way they can understand. The Bible says not to provoke our children to anger. It tells us to train them up as we go through our days. If you are struggling with a strong-willed child, I would encourage you to read up on the Love Languages and the Languages of Apology. Your struggle may be as simple as not speaking the same love language, and therefore, they don't feel loved and act out.

I would also encourage you to take a hard look at your parenting style. Strong wills can easily be redirected if you are careful in the way you manage the situation. I learned not to pick a battle, but I never backed down from one if one of the kids decided to pick one. I also learned not to micro-manage my littles too much, especially the boys. Their little selves need to feel big sometimes.

Your mission, should you choose to except it, is to discover what makes them tick, what thrills and fills their hearts, and to train them to WANT to behave within the boundaries of acceptable behavior in your home.

Mommy, you got this!!

Mommy Moment...

Mommies everywhere dream of the people their children will become. They imagine them to be handsome men and beautiful women. They see them as successful Doctors and Lawyers. They may imagine them as business owners or CEOs. But what is it that we really want for our children?

Material wealth is certainly nice, as is social status, but is it what we really want for our kids? I think what we truly want is for them to be amazing adults, strong in their faith, joyful, solid in their convictions, honest, hard-working, compassionate, gentle hearted yet wise and discerning.

It's character that we truly want. --Mine are certainly characters, but that's not the same thing. LOL-- How do we raise them up to have character?

My parents were a part of the generation we call the "Greatest Generation." They were men and women of character. I think we would do well to look back and see how they were raised to help answer the question. Life was hard for them. Nothing was given to them that they did not work hard to earn. They had to help care for their siblings. They weren't Idols to be given an allowance just for being part of the family, no extravagant gifts or parties, no car simply for turning 16. Many of them went to work for a neighbor or friend at a young age and gave that money over to their parents to help feed the family. Their mothers expected a lot from them. They weren't "mini me's" to be dolled up and nearly worshiped, instead they were individuals to be trained, loved and cared for.

Children are not idols to bow to, nor trophies to show off to your friends. They are God given responsibilities.

Sweet Mommy, I am in no way scolding or judging. I am trying to help you raise amazing children who become amazing adults. It is so easy to slide from wanting to be mother into wanting to be friend. I know! I have been there. In making life easier for our children, we accidentally take from them the very things they NEED. They need challenges, so they can learn to overcome. They need responsibilities, to learn to work hard. They need hard work, so they can be proud of their efforts. It is hard to watch them struggle. But in those struggles they learn to cry out to God for help. And actually... isn't that the most important thing we can teach them? Crying out to God, loving Him, following Him, those are the things that will make them truly successful.

Mommy, you got this!!

Mommy Moment...

I just want to take a moment to recognize daddies. The statistics tell us that children who grow up in a traditional home with a mommy and a daddy do better in school and in life. Prison stats tell us that daddies make all the difference in the world. Kids get into less trouble when they have an active dad present. If we honor their daddy, they will too. If we degrade them or openly disagree with them, they will too.

Danielle and I were in a Bible study together a few years back when her family was living here. I don't remember the study topic, but for some reason Danielle said she had never heard Curt and I argue. The ladies laughed. Then they were astonished that she was earnest. She had not ever heard us argue... still hasn't. She HAS seen me frustrated, but I have always deferred to Curt. We might discuss the subject later, but not ever in front of the kids.

Some will say it isn't healthy to not argue, but I would disagree. Kids see and hear arguing in everyday life at school, on TV, and with friends. I never felt the need to teach them to argue. I did feel, however, the need to teach them to control their emotional outbursts and to use logic to state their opinions. Our society, in general, doesn't honor dads. TV shows portray dads as bumbling idiots. On most commercials its either the mom, or even the child, who is the smart one. Dads are put down terribly.

It wasn't so in our home. Curt may be the quiet one, but he is certainly not put down or looked down upon. He makes all the final decisions. He sets the schedule. He is our provider and protector... and I am THRILLED with my role as the mommy! I tried to honor Curt because I wanted the kids to honor and adore their daddy.

I wanted them to play hard with him. I wanted them to work hard with Him. I wanted them to turn to him when they have a problem and listen to his wisdom. Sweet mommy, it is important that they appreciate the fathers that they have. Mine was taken by death far too soon. I will miss that gruff old man till the day I die. We never know how much time we have. I wanted my kids to have the best memories of their dad that they could have. Those memories will help hold them steady in life.

Men today have a tough job. Society sends them all sorts of confusing messages. Daddies are amazing! I hope you take the time to honor your own dad and teach your kids to honor their dad as well.

Mommy, you got this!!

Mommy Moment...

There have been numerous times when I couldn't see how God could fix a situation, or I wasn't sure He would even want to. Often, I wasn't totally sure if I really heard His voice, and yet I have seen Him do so many things in my life, big and little.

I was out visiting Danielle when Kristi was just a baby. Matthew was only 2 or 3, and Jeff had been deployed. We hated to see Danielle be all alone for the whole time he was gone, so off I went, across the country to Washington State. It was a great visit. Dani introduced me to her friends. She took me to her church. We walked to the lake across the road from her. We spent time playing games with Matthew. It was marvelous!

Matthew had learned to call me on Danielle's phone, so he felt like he knew me. I wasn't a stranger to him. I was his friend and Granny. Each morning he and I would play or walk around the lake so that Danielle and the baby could sleep a little. He was such a little man.

When I met one of Danielle's friends, I felt like I should do something nice for her. I could not explain why I felt that way. I just kept thinking I should buy her a certain book; one she had mentioned. The problem was…I had no money. Our budget was stretched as far as it would go just to get me out to see Dani. How was I ever going to afford that book? It was like $20 (which is not much…unless you have nothing).

Well, Matthew and I were out for a walk early Sunday morning. It was too early to start breakfast, so we wandered down to the lake. We enjoyed the little park by the dock. As we looked into the crystal-clear water, I began to see something shiny, really shiny. As we peered into the lake, we realized we were looking at money! Quarters, nickels, and dimes. Then, I could not believe what I saw... $20 dollar bills! Not kidding! There were all sorts of money mixed into the sand just under the dock.

You might wonder what I did. Well, much to the horror of my little grandson, I walked out into the chest-high water and fished out all the money I could! Poor little Matthew was astonished that I would break the rules and go into the lake. See, he had been told to stay out of the water, and I had just broken the rule! He was so shocked. He lectured me the whole way back to the house!

Did I mention it was a MOUNTAIN lake? A COLD mountain lake? Really cold!

Anyhow... God provided. I bought the book and had extra cash to treat Dani and the kids. God is amazing!

Mommy, you got this!!

Mommy Moment...

I began to be aware of just how much junk food and sugar we ate when our son was little. I cooked 3 meals every day, with very few exceptions, but we still consumed way too much junk. I began to make changes. Those changes made a huge difference in the kids' behavior. At about the same time I realized how many chemicals we give our kids, sugar substitutes, medicines, and such. We rub them down with lotions after baths and chemical sunscreens before they go outside. When they have a scraped knee, an antibiotic cream is applied. –WOW!!

Slowly I began to make more changes. I spent time studying anatomy and how the body is designed to heal itself. It's truly fascinating! I quite enjoyed the new knowledge I acquired. –An old dog CAN learn new tricks!

I found this amazing healing salve for wounds of all sort. It was made of olive oil and herbs with a little bee's wax to make it semi-solid. Problem was, it was PRICEY! Like $30 for 4 ounces! Ouch! So, I began making it. It took a few tries. -- Like many of my cooking adventures, the first few batches didn't work so well.

My first batch was far to solid, like a super hard bar of soap. Not quite like rubbing a rock on your skin, but close. The next one was better. I decreased the amount of bee's wax considerably. I felt so good about my efforts, but the fragrance of the herbs was not a favorite with my kids, so the next time I tried adding a little essential oil…much better.

Believe it or not, l used that same salve on my old milk cow. We never had any issues with her utter or mastitis, but once she got into some wire. It left her with a 4-inch gash on her utter. I didn't see it for a few days. By the time I noticed, it was festering and infected. I slathered that salve on her for the next couple of days and within 24 hours the redness, swelling and tenderness was completely gone!!

Our eldest daughter improved the recipe and began marketing that salve. She started quite a little business. She sells that and other herbal remedies online and at vender fairs. I think it's awesome that God took my desire for a better product and turned it into a business for Danielle.

God will bless your efforts, Sweet Mommy. Even if they don't turn out quite right at first. Don't give up. Start over. Laugh at your mistakes. He will honor your desire to be a great mommy. –If I can do this, and still end up with amazing children, you will have no trouble. If you have a bad day just re-read a few of my stories, and you will be encouraged!

Mommy, you got this!!

Mommy Moment...

I got a call one afternoon. It was one of the hired hands at the farm. They NEVER call so I knew it wasn't good. "Curt fell off the top of the truck. I will bring him home."

Just so you know, a "truck" is not a pickup, it is an actual farm truck. Similar to the semis you see on the highway, but the trailer section is completely open on the top. It has to be open -like a dump truck- so that the commodities can be blown in or dumped into the back. They are close to twenty feet high. Curt had been working on one preparing it for harvest.

When the farm hand brought him in, I was a bit shocked. His face was all cut up. He was coherent, but he sure looked a mess. He had been on the top and fell onto the cement below. Right on his face!

Have you ever seen a John Wayne movie? The men on those movies are tough! If they get shot, they'd have a friend dig the bullet out while they watched. If someone is stabbed, the wife goes out to the horse and pulls some hair from the tail and stitches up the wound. They set their own broken bones. They are hard core men.

Well, Curt laid down on the couch. I cleaned his wounds the best I could. Then I asked him if he wanted to go to the hospital. "Nope. You can do this."

Ahhh! Me! Ummm...

"Just do the best you can," He said calmly.

I did. He kept encouraging me and I kept cleaning and bandaging. The worst of it was his right cheek. I lifted the skin on his cheek and cleaned under it the best I could. I got the butterfly bandages out to hold the skin in place.

I was shaking so badly. I couldn't believe that he thought I was capable of dealing with this. I had to make myself take deep breaths and focus on what I was doing. I could never have been a nurse. I was fine while I was working. I stayed calm and did what needed to be done. But then...

I finished bandaging his wounds, kissed the top of his head, walked to our bathroom and collapsed on the floor. I thought for a minute I would pass out. Instead, I just sat there and cried. Once the fear and adrenaline left me, I was calm again and I went to sit with Curt. -He is a tough ol' guy.

You never know what you are capable of until you are forced to push yourself.

Mommy, you got this!!

Mommy Moment...

Over the years Curt came home with a wide selection of animals, everything from the turtles who became permanent pets, to little blue-tailed skinks (lizards) that were NOT welcome to stay.

When he would come home and say, "I found something," or "go look in the back of the pickup," we all perked up. It was a bit like town kids hearing the music from an ice cream truck. We dropped what we were doing and ran to him. He brought us snapping turtles, ground owls, moles, voles, baby birds, baby bunnies, and of course the sand turtles and lizards that I have written about. The little animals were returned to their homes unharmed, except the sand turtles. They were put into the chicken yard, where they became our pets.

Curt used those little animals to teach our kids many things. He taught them to respect nature. He taught them to respect life. He taught them compassion. They learned to be wary of wild animals after looking at the claws on the moles, and the clenching power in a snapping turtles jaw. They learned of the wonderful diversity in the animals God created and how important each animal type is to our environment. It was a bit of a biology lab in our front yard.

There are many of you sweet mommies who are considering home education. I would encourage you to do so. We loved it! Not all our teaching was done from a schoolbook. I would dare to say that the most important things we taught were NOT found there at all. We used the Bible as our foundation, and the creation around us as our laboratory. Teaching at home gave us time to explore the world around us together. That was the key.

Our favorite lessons were the ones we learned together; cooking, sewing, feeding orphaned kittens, or maybe watching a snapping turtle break a good-sized stick with its jaw. Learning as a family can be such a blessing!

Mommy, you got this!!

Mommy Moment...

I am convinced that adolescence is a tough time for most kids. It is the times when their brains begin to accept abstract thoughts, their bodies are changing physically, and hormones are being produced at a rapid rate. With all of that comes an emotional roller-coaster. Add in all the societal pressure to look just right and to conform to their peers, and they have quite the challenge just to survive each day emotionally.

I was no different. I struggled to find my place. My parents were older and weren't overly attentive or aware of what was happening to me. I had no one to share my insecurities with, no guidance as to what my body was about to go through.

I remember being about 10, maybe 11, when I was given a little bikini swimsuit in a box of hand-me-downs from a neighbor. Now, it was nothing like bikinis today. It had a full, high waisted bottom and the top looked more like a workout bra of today. What it did have was a few rows of tiny ruffles on the front. I had never worn a bikini, but I spent all summer long in the city pool. I had noticed that other girls had a shape. I did not. Other girls enjoyed the attention of the boys. I did not. Somehow my little brain took in all that information and decided it was a grand idea to wear that bikini top inside out.

Yes, I really did. I wore it that way under my clothes for a bit, but then I wore it that way even at the pool.

Yes, I was a socially awkward child.

No one said anything. No one seemed to notice. Not my friend. Not my parents. I continued to wear it that way for the entire summer.

I wish I could go back and talk to that little girl. I wish I could tell her the words she never heard. I would tell her that she was beautiful.

I would tell her that her body would change at its own rate, that the girls who were tall and shapely now were just getting a head start, and that she would catch up one day. I would tell her that she had special gifts to share with this world that no one else has. I would tell her that she was precious and did not need to fit in with the others. Mostly I would tell her to look to God and He would show her all the beauty He placed in her heart.

I tried to tell my own kids those things. They still had to find their own place and go through their own insecurities, but they knew that God loved them dearly and I did too. I pray that you know that, too.

Mommy, you got this!!

Mommy moment...

When Devin was little, we had a bunch of friends and family tell us all the time that he was hyperactive. They all said it with a smile, but they were serious and, at times, quite mean about it. The more I heard it the stronger this feeling of protective momma bear became.

I am quite serious. It began to really upset me. I was to the point of telling people to "back off, he is fine!" The indignation would rise in my heart and I would want to sass back and be rude to them.

I know. It wasn't the right thing, but I was young and really didn't know how to deal with their hurtful words. But, thankfully, I did not accept them. I refused to even consider that his busy body and active mind were somehow a bad thing. I did study ADHD and ADD. I did educate myself on the topic, but I did NOT accept that it meant something was wrong with Devin.

I changed his diet a bit. I watched his sugar intake. I gave him plenty of time outside to explore and imagine. And...I prayed!

I prayed and prayed, for him, for his mind and for his heart. I prayed that their words would not settle into his heart. I prayed that God would protect him from the cruel word...intended or not...they were cruel.

God answered those prayers in oh so many ways! I found the books I needed that encouraged me to stand up for Devin. I heard programs on the radio about busy boys. But, the coolest thing I found was a Christian Comedian who had several routines on the subject. He had been labeled ADD, and he used it to teach people that it was not a bad thing. Devin heard those routines over and over. -- I am so grateful to that comedian.

People can be cruel. Their words can settle into a child's heart. As mommies we are the warriors who are stationed to protect our children.

We also must be careful that we don't OVER protect.

I did NOT let Devin behave badly just because he was busy. He wasn't allowed to be rude, demanding or defiant. I was certainly his defender, but NOT his enabler. It is a fine line at times. I begged God for wisdom! I knew I could have easily become the mom you erred on the wrong side of the line and raised an out-of-control brat. I didn't want THAT either.

I think I cried over that sweet baby boy more than I cried over the others, probably because I was young and overwhelmed at the task of motherhood, but also because I had begun to see just how important my roll was. Sweet Mommy, your task is daunting, but your roll is VITAL. Your children need you to be their warrior, their trainer, their nurturer. It will take all you have within you.

You may not have the costume, but you are Wonder Woman!

Mommy, you got this!!

Mommy Moment...

My walk as a Christian and my journey as a mother are closely tied. I was 18 when they both began, so they are intertwined and difficult to separate. God used motherhood to pull me to Him and my faith guided everything I did as a mommy. No, I did not get everything right. Yes, I made hundreds of wrong turns or emotional decisions, but I clung to God and returned to Him every time I got off track.

When Devin was just 2 I had this overwhelming feeling that he would grow up to be a prayer warrior. I know that sounds a bit strange. I found it strange at the time. Each time I prayed for my little guy, I felt God say he would be a prayer warrior. I felt compelled to continually pray for wisdom as his mother, because I didn't want to mess that up. I didn't want my shortcomings and sin to stop God's plan for that little boy. It kept me humble and in prayer.

As Devin grew, I didn't tell him what I felt God had told me. God would reveal Himself to Devin at the right time. I did all I could to encourage a strong faith in God through books and tapes, and through our daily lives. We talked about faith and about God all the time.

God brought many opportunities to Devin. We would be at a gathering and the adult in charge would turn to him and ask him to pray... like everywhere we went, church gatherings, 4-H meetings, family gatherings. People would just ask him to pray. At times, he would get frustrated with them. THEY were adults, why would they ask him, a teen, to pray for the group? I think God was giving him those opportunities. He traveled with me to a Josh McDowell seminar once. It was a gathering of several hundred youth leaders and pastors. Mr. McDowell come over to our table and visited with us a bit…and asked Devin to pray.

My fears and insecurities could have been my excuse to pull back and shelter Devin. His ADHD behavior could have been an excuse to become frustrated and try to "reign in" that little boy, or to give him meds and have him labeled as ADD/ ADHD. Either of those could have destroyed to spirit that God had given him. I was hard on him. I did expect a great deal of good behavior from a little busy boy. Not, because I wanted to control or hold him back, but because God created him to RUN!! He was created to lead and guide others. He would become a great prayer warrior if I did NOT get in the way.

God has a lot to say about parenting in the Bible. There are examples of humble Godly mothers and examples of awful parents. There are guidelines and there is hope written in The Word. I desperately clung to those words and tried to live what they said.

I have used Devin as my example here, but ALL children have a calling. ALL children are of utmost importance to God. They each have a special gift and are precious to God. I believe EVERY child has a place in God's Kingdom. As a mommy, it is our job to lead them to God and teach them to hear His voice. God will do the rest.

Mommy, you got this!!

There are so many more things I wish I could share with you. I hope you have found joy, encouragement and hope in my stories.

I watched the movie "I Still Believe." The lead female character has a line in it that really touched my heart. She says that her pain and suffering will have been worth it if it helps even ***one*** person. I so understand that heart felt statement. If these stories have helped even just one of you, then all of the struggle and mess, all of the zany silliness would be worth it.

Sweet Mommies, that's why I have written these stories from my life. I pray that they help you in your own life.

I pray that someway somehow my life will bring you hope, and that you have seen the love, the power, and the grace of God as you have read these stories. He is real, and He adores you!

May God be with you!

You got this!!

Made in the USA
Middletown, DE
06 January 2022

57928960R00137